TABLE OF C

D0978185

Background: Shiprock Trading Post. From top: Seedshaman;
Holly Modine Studio; RT Davis Shepherd and Handweaver;
Española Valley Fiber Arts Center.

TABLE OF CONTENTS

From top: Karen Martinez Studio and Gallery;
Doc Campbell's Post/Gila Country Corner Gallery;
Tapestry Gallery; Northern New Mexico College Fiber
Arts Program.

ON THE COVER: *Navajo "Eyedazzler" serape,*
Germantown yarn (detail of weaving),
c. 1890. Shiprock Trading Post.
Photography by Diane Bowman, Laura Marcus,
Charmeine Wait, Claude Stephenson, Carol Cooper,
and trails sites. Page 30 © Jack Parsons.

THE NEW MEXICO FIBER ARTS TRAILS

NEW MEXICO ARTS
A Division of the
Department of Cultural Affairs

Loie Fecteau, *Executive Director*
Carol Cooper, *Project Manager*
Doug Patinka, *DCA Webmaster*
Laura Marcus, *Writer/Researcher*
Diane Bowman, *Northern New Mexico
Regional Coordinator*
Charmeine Wait, *Southern New Mexico
Regional Coordinator*
Mary Sweitzer, *Designer*
Cheryle Mano Mitchell, *Editor*
Glen Strock, *Map Illustrator*
Bette Bradbury, *WESST Corp.,
Workshops Coordinator*

SPECIAL THANKS TO
OUR INVALUABLE PARTNERS:
New Mexico Fiber Artisans
Steering Committee
Regional Development Corp.
Empowering Business
Spirit Initiative
New Mexico Women's Foundation
And our many supporters

NEW MEXICO ARTS STAFF
Lisa Peinado, *Operations Director*
Loretta Chama,
Contracts Administrator
Ann Weisman,
Program Coordinator
Ruth Lommel, *Administrator*
Anna Blyth,
Public Information Officer
Claude Stephenson,
State Folklorist
Laurie Wilder,
IS Database Administrator

DEPARTMENT OF CULTURAL AFFAIRS
Stuart A. Ashman,
Cabinet Secretary
Anne Green-Romig,
Director of Legislative Affairs
Doug Svetnicka,
Communications Director
Sue Sturtevant,
Director of Statewide Partnerships
Maggie Coffey-Pilcher,
General Counsel

Governor Bill Richardson
First Lady Barbara Richardson
Lt. Governor Diane Denish
New Mexico Legislature
New Mexico Arts Commission
led by Chair Janice Spence
and Vice Chair Herb Denish

Contact: New Mexico Arts, PO Box 1450,
Santa Fe, New Mexico, 87504-1450.
Tel: 505 827-6490; 1-800-879-4278
(Instate); www.nmarts.org;
www.nmfiberarts.org

NEW MEXICO FIBER ARTS TRAILS

THE VISION

A RTISTS NEED OPPORTUNITIES TO MAKE A living at home. This is the simple answer to "Why the New Mexico Fiber Arts Trails?" The arts trails evolved from New Mexico Arts' leadership in nurturing arts entrepreneurship. We believe arts-based economic development is vital to a sustainable future for our state's rural communities.

Our inspiration was the resounding success of HandMade in America's western North Carolina Craft Heritage Trails and its visionary founder Becky Anderson. She jumpstarted our gathering of rural cultural tourism advocates in August 2005. Participating fiber artists wove a tale that called out for fiber arts trails. The New Mexico Fiber Artisans coalition born at that meeting became invaluable trail planning partners. A grassroots campaign resulted in Governor Bill Richardson and the New Mexico Legislature funding New Mexico Arts to create statewide arts trails – the first of hopefully a series. We have many to thank.

So why fiber arts? They are universal yet local, democratic and accessible. They encompass rich and age-old cultural traditions, spin over the edges into fresh contemporary work, and zigzag everywhere. No matter the artistic form, they require structure but demand innovation and freedom, often of both artist and admirer.

And why trails? Because creativity flourishes on the back roads, for both artists and travelers. The trails celebrate New Mexico's diverse communities, lifestyles, and landscapes. They reveal the natural world that inspires, nurtures, and supplies fiber-related activities. The trails traverse an integrated cycle - from raw materials through a medley of techniques and creative processes to hand-crafted works of art – and heart.

Enjoy! The work of more than 200 New Mexico fiber artists awaits you at 71 destinations along the trails. We invite you to support creativity at its source. Welcome to the rich textures of New Mexico fiber!

Loie Fecteau
Executive Director, New Mexico Arts

Carol Cooper
Project Manager, New Mexico Arts

TRAVELING THE TRAILS

NEW MEXICO IS HOME TO A REMARK-able diversity of fiber artists who create and present their work in varied settings. The New Mexico Fiber Arts Trails are a collaboration between New Mexico Arts and a grassroots network of fiber artists to cultivate awareness of our rich and unique fiber arts heritage, as well as opportunities for artists to prosper in their home communities. Sites appearing in the New Mexico Fiber Arts Trails Guide have participated in an application process and are ready for company.

Some sites are collectives, representing multiple local artists, while others are working farms or studios, galleries, museums, suppliers, and more. Inevitably, there are many New Mexico-based fiber artists and businesses not listed on the trails, leaving plenty of room for discovery along the way. We hope this guide will be a springboard for – dare we say it? – woolly adventures! Due to space limitations, guide entries offer only a glimpse of trail sites. Many have tantalizing Web sites where you can learn more before embarking on the Fiber Arts Trails.

We have organized the Trails by region: North Central, Northwest, and South. Within these loops, you will find spurs, inviting you to venture on your own itinerary. So, remember to pack a good map of New Mexico and hit the Trails!

Background: Earth Arts. Above: Julie Wagner Studio.

TIPS

A few things to make your trip the best it can be:

- **ENJOY THE WIDE OPEN SPACES**
  This is a rural guide, inviting you to wander off the beaten path and explore New Mexico's back roads. The Trails meander through diverse ecosystems, but our dry climate and high elevation are constants through-out. Be sure to bring plenty of water. Fill your tank before heading out on long stretches of open road, as gas pumps can be few and far between, and some rural areas do not have cell phone reception. Sites indicated by ☎ are located on dirt or gravel roads where access may be challenging, especially after rain or snow. A call ahead to site hosts for advice will give you peace of mind. In winter months especially, check all road conditions and weather forecasts before striking out on the Trails.

- **FOOD AND LODGING** New Mexico is a traveler's paradise, with local eateries and accommodations aplenty. Ask your Fiber Arts Trails hosts for recommendations for those fabulous, out-of-the-way places. Some sites offer their own lodging, an added treat!

- **TAKE YOUR TIME** The fiber arts invite us to take time out, to create, to observe, to run fingers over sumptuous textures, to call on passionate people with stories to tell, to meet charming fiber animals, and to under-stand fiber processes – from fleece to finish. Leave yourself time to visit with hosts, travel scenic byways, explore local attractions, and lose yourself in the Land of Enchantment.

- **HOURS** Fiber Arts Trails site hours of operation vary, with some sites closed Sundays or for major holidays or for entire seasons. Even if open, some sites have limited hours or are open by appointment, welcoming visitors at other times. Weather may also affect hours, so check hours of operation carefully! If there is a site you're hoping to visit, or if it's some distance away, it never hurts to call ahead.

- **HONOR YOUR FURRY HOSTS** If you are traveling with pets, please do not bring them to Fiber Arts Trails sites, out of consideration for the animals who live – and work – along the Trails.
- **VISITORS WITH SPECIAL NEEDS** Sites vary in accessibility. Wheelchair accessible sites are indicated by ♿. Sites with wheelchair accessible restrooms are designated by ♿. Sites without wheelchair accessible restrooms often are located near public facilities. It's best to call ahead to sites on your itinerary to confirm specific accommodations.

Peloncillo Mountains, near Rodeo

- **TRAILS FOR ALL TO ENJOY** The Fiber Arts Trails will have special appeal for fiber artists and aficionados, and we anticipate there will be converts along the way. Young people will relish the occasion to learn about – or even try – fiber arts processes themselves, or visit with fiber animals. Sites carrying fiber arts supplies ✄ and those offering classes or workshops 🍎 are ideal for indulging your fiber arts passions. Because the trails traverse stunning landscapes, many with public access, hiking, camping, skiing, cycling, fishing, birdwatching, and more – and areas of great cultural, historical, and archaeological interest – we heartily believe there is something for everyone on the New Mexico Fiber Arts Trails. Happy trails! ✳

USEFUL INFORMATION FOR TRAVELERS

- **CHECK THE NETWORK** As we go to press, site entry information is current. To accommodate the inevitable – change, that is – two trail hosts are serving as **FIBER NETWORK** sites, where travelers can stay informed. For Fiber Arts Trails updates in northern or northwestern New Mexico, stop by or call the Española Valley Fiber Arts Center at 505.747.3577, or in the south, The Common Thread in Silver City, 505.538.5733. New Mexico is slated to add new area codes; keep this in mind as you dial.

- **NEW MEXICO TOURISM DEPARTMENT** A wealth of information for travelers: cultural and historical highlights, including New Mexico Indian Tourism, Scenic Byways, State Parks and Monuments, events calendars, maps, and more helpful information. newmexico.org | 800.545.2070

- **INDIAN COUNTRY NEW MEXICO** Additional information about the state's Native communities. IndianCountryNM.org

- **ROAD CONDITIONS AND WEATHER** nmroads.com 800.432.4269 | AM radio 1610

- **NEW MEXICO STATE POLICE** 505.827.9300

CALENDAR OF EVENTS

Throughout the year, New Mexico is rich with events that feature fiber arts. Below is a listing of only some of the fiber arts activities around the state. Contact New Mexico Fiber Arts Trails site hosts, local fiber arts guilds, and other arts and civic organizations for information about activities in their neighborhoods. New Mexico is also home to many studio tours that often feature fiber arts. For a detailed listing, visit the Albuquerque Arts Alliance at abqarts.org/resources/studiotours.htm.

CROWNPOINT RUG AUCTION
mttaylor.com/rug-auction
505.786.7386
An institution since 1968, this community-based event features a diverse selection of Navajo rugs. It's held at the Crownpoint Elementary School, generally the third Friday evening of **every month;** check Web site for exact dates.

NEW MEXICO WOMEN'S FOUNDATION RAG RUG FESTIVALS
nmwf.org/events.html
505.983.6155
The New Mexico Women's Foundation holds Rag Rug Festivals around the state to exhibit and market the weaving and other fiber arts

of their grantee organizations and individual artists. **March,** Las Cruces, New Mexico Farm & Ranch Heritage Museum; **August,** Santa Fe, Udall Center for Museum Resources, Museum Hill; **November,** Farmington, Farmington Museum at Gateway Park.

QUILT SHOWS
quiltguilds.com/new_mexico.htm
New Mexico is home to regional quilt guilds, many that hold regular shows and events, among them the Festival of Quilts in Hobbs, held the first two weeks in **May.** Contact: arleenwcoleson@aol.com.

BIENNIAL ALBUQUERQUE FIBER ARTS FIESTA
fiberartsfiesta.org
Held biannually over Memorial Day weekend in **May** at the Creative Arts Building, EXPO New Mexico, home of the NM State Fair. Hosted by the Albuquerque Fiber Arts Council, a coalition of local fiber arts guilds, this event has a vendors mall, demonstrations, workshops, and more – all under one roof.

EL RANCHO DE LAS GOLONDRINAS
golondrinas.org
Learn about Spanish colonial fiber arts in context at this living history museum, situated in an 18th-century rancho in La Cienega that served as a way station along the historic Camino Real. Traditional fiber arts

Background: Terrazas Traditional Arts. From top: Ramah Navajo Weavers Association; The Common Thread; Thunder Creek Quilt Company; Furniture and More.

demonstrations every Friday, **June – October**. Check Web site for calendar of special events.

SOUTHWEST REGIONAL SPINNERS RETREAT
fiberartscollective.org/guildsorgs.html.
Based in Las Cruces, the Southwest Regional Spinners meet in the Sacramento Mountains for an annual retreat/workshop in **July**.

SPANISH MARKET
spanishmarket.org
505.983.2226
Held the last full weekend in **July** in the Santa Fe Plaza, a celebration and market of the unique artistic heritage of Hispanic New Mexico and Colorado, featuring many fiber art forms. Winter Market held in downtown Santa Fe in **December**.

SANTA FE INDIAN MARKET
swaia.org   505.983.5220
The Southwestern Association for Indian Arts sponsors this premier event

every **August** that includes work by Native American fiber artists. Winter Showcase held in downtown Santa Fe in **November**.

SHEEP TO SHAWL, NEW MEXICO STATE FAIR
lasaranas.org/sheep_to_shawl.htm
Held in **September** as part of the New Mexico State Fair in Albuquerque. A collaborative project of Las Arañas Spinners and Weavers Guild and the New Mexico Wool Growers with a demonstration area showing all phases from raw sheep fleece to finished items and featuring a gallery of handmade fiber arts. The State Fair also has other fiber arts displays and demonstrations.

TAOS WOOL FESTIVAL
www.taoswoolfestival.org
Held the first full weekend in **October**, sponsored by the Mountain and Valley Wool Association. A celebration of wool in all imaginable forms, including regional traditional and contemporary fiber arts, yarn and tools, books,

demonstrations and workshops, vendors' booths, and fiber critter display.

BEST OF THE SOUTHWEST FIBER ARTS FESTIVAL
woolfestivalsw.meridan1.net
505.325.2837
Held in **November** at the McGee Park Convention Center in Farmington, this multicultural, regional event features fiber arts and supplies vendors, demonstrations, workshops, competitions, an auction, and more! ✳

From top: Taos Pueblo land and Taos Mountain; Española Valley Fiber Arts Center; Centinela Traditional Arts; also Centinela.

You have the Río Grande. On top of that was the indigenous acequia system. Then the Spaniards came into different portions of the state and enhanced what was already here. New Mexico is also a major flyway for birds and geese – the water and the flora accompany that. Roads in cities are overlaid with freeways following those major routes. And so, we identify with that. The idea of trails is still part of the contemporary vocabulary, even though we don't see the original – it's like a historic X-ray.

—RAMONA SAKIESTEWA
CONTEMPORARY FIBER ARTIST
2006 GOVERNOR'S AWARD FOR EXCELLENCE IN THE ARTS

NORTH CENTRAL LOOP

To the north, back roads beckon, weaving along river valleys, winding through velvet mountains and red rock canyons sculpted by time, crossing plains that stretch as far as the eye can see. The land speaks in textures. Sage, golden chamisa, violet asters, and grasses cover the earth in a blanket of natural hues.

Billowing clouds roll across the heavens like lengths of wool roving ready to spin against a cobalt sky. The ever-shifting light shimmers with creativity that lives in the very air we breathe. Geology carves designs for the eye to behold, and imaginations and fingers transform what we see into useful and beautiful items.

New Mexico fiber arts grow organically from the land and the cultures it nurtures. The people are as varied as the landscape: Pueblo communities with roots growing deep into the soil, centuries-old Hispanic villages tucked into fertile valleys, artist communities re-inhabiting abandoned mining and mill towns. Their stories are an interwoven tapestry, built row upon row into striking patterns, at once familiar and new. Visit home studios, long-established workshops, yarn emporiums brimming with color and inspiration, fiber farms inhabited by fleece-covered creatures, galleries abundant with local treasure, a farm resplendent with dye plants, community centers built around fiber arts. If you're moved to nurture your own creativity, the materials and willing teachers are close at hand. ✳

Background: Black Mesa, San Ildefonso Pueblo. Inset: Los Vigiles Living Traditions Fiber Studio & Supply.

[NORTH CENTRAL]

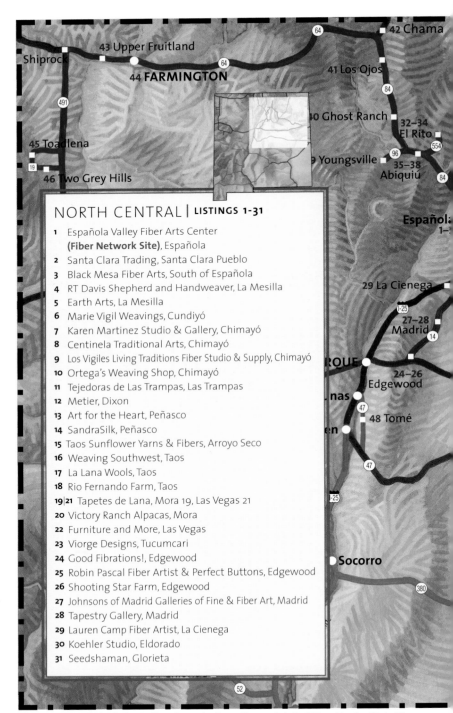

43 Upper Fruitland

Shiprock

64

42 Chama

44 **FARMINGTON**

41 Los Ojos

84

491

40 Ghost Ranch

32–34
El Rito

45 Toadlena

554

19

96

39 Youngsville

35–38
Abiquiú

84

46 Two Grey Hills

Española
1–

NORTH CENTRAL | LISTINGS 1-31

1 Española Valley Fiber Arts Center
   (Fiber Network Site), Española
2 Santa Clara Trading, Santa Clara Pueblo
3 Black Mesa Fiber Arts, South of Española
4 RT Davis Shepherd and Handweaver, La Mesilla
5 Earth Arts, La Mesilla
6 Marie Vigil Weavings, Cundiyó
7 Karen Martinez Studio & Gallery, Chimayó
8 Centinela Traditional Arts, Chimayó
9 Los Vigiles Living Traditions Fiber Studio & Supply, Chimayó
10 Ortega's Weaving Shop, Chimayó
11 Tejedoras de Las Trampas, Las Trampas
12 Metier, Dixon
13 Art for the Heart, Peñasco
14 SandraSilk, Peñasco
15 Taos Sunflower Yarns & Fibers, Arroyo Seco
16 Weaving Southwest, Taos
17 La Lana Wools, Taos
18 Rio Fernando Farm, Taos
19|21 Tapetes de Lana, Mora 19, Las Vegas 21
20 Victory Ranch Alpacas, Mora
22 Furniture and More, Las Vegas
23 Viorge Designs, Tucumcari
24 Good Fibrations!, Edgewood
25 Robin Pascal Fiber Artist & Perfect Buttons, Edgewood
26 Shooting Star Farm, Edgewood
27 Johnsons of Madrid Galleries of Fine & Fiber Art, Madrid
28 Tapestry Gallery, Madrid
29 Lauren Camp Fiber Artist, La Cienega
30 Koehler Studio, Eldorado
31 Seedshaman, Glorieta

29 La Cienega

I-25

27–28
Madrid

14

RQUE

24–26
Edgewood

nas

47

48 Tomé

en

47

I-25

Socorro

380

52

Map not to scale; includes trail routes only. Consult your detailed New Mexico State Map.

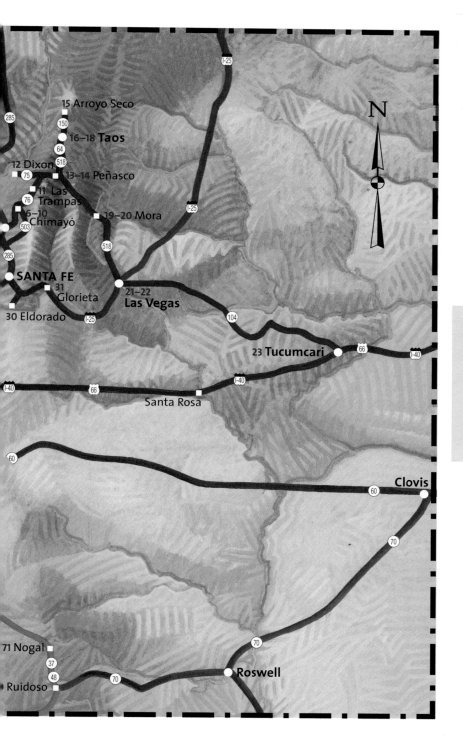

N

15 Arroyo Seco

285

150

16–18 **Taos**

64

12 Dixon 518

75   13–14 Peñasco

11 Las
Trampas
76

6–10
Chimayó
503

19–20 Mora

I-25

285

518

SANTA FE

31
Glorieta

21–22
Las Vegas

30 Eldorado I-25

104

23 **Tucumcari** 66 I-40

I-40 66

Santa Rosa I-40

60

60 **Clovis**

70

71 Nogal

37

48 70

Ruidoso

70 **Roswell**

PUEBLO FIBER ARTS

CONTINUITY AND CHANGE

Santa Clara Trading

AS EARLY AS A.D. 200, THE MOGOLLON OF southern New Mexico and the Anasazi to the north – ancestors of today's Pueblo peoples – used off-loom techniques to craft items from plant fibers, human and animal hair, fur, and feathers. New Mexico's arid climate has allowed the survival of an extraordinary range of prehistoric fiber arts – sandals, straps and bags, netting, rope, clothing, baskets, mats, and more – many woven in intricate techniques and designs. The cultivation of cotton and the development of the upright loom brought woven cloth to prominence as a central feature of Pueblo daily and ceremonial life, and as a valued intercultural trade commodity. The arrival of the Spanish in the late-16th century brought far-reaching changes in Pueblo life, including wool for weaving.

Fiber arts remain an essential feature of Pueblo cere-monial life, including feast days when dancers wear embroidered kilts and mantas as well as loomed sashes and hair ties, and crocheted leggings. Unlike other Southwest Native art forms, Pueblo fiber arts have always been made almost exclusively for community use, maintaining a connection to their cultural roots in the agricultural cycle that is at the heart of ceremonial practice. Contemporary fiber arts designs are strikingly similar to patterns on kilts and sashes worn by dancers depicted in kiva murals from hundreds of years ago. As in many cultures, fiber arts are a barometer of change – and continuity. ✻

They say you can't be all things to all people, but Española Valley Fiber Arts Center (EVFAC) comes close. In 1995, the sight of looms gathering dust was a call to action for a handful of dedi-cated weavers. EVFAC has blossomed into a vibrant nonprofit organization and community that promotes fiber arts and supports 400 members as artists and entre-preneurs. Opportunities to acquire skills, create prod-ucts, and earn income are realized through 30 floor looms; work space for myriad classes; a dye kitchen; a fiber arts library; and a top-notch gallery of felted items; Río Grande, Navajo, and rag rugs; wearable art; and more. In its historic quarters, EVFAC car-ries fiber, yarn, and supplies, much of it locally produced. Sign up for a class or drop by for spinning or knitting.

M, 9-8; T-SA, 9-5; SU, 12-5
505.747.3577 evfac.org
info@evfac.org
From Santa Fe, north on Hwy 84/285. Enter Española on Riverside Dr. At third light, turn left on Paseo de Oñate. Go over Río Grande bridge. EVFAC is fourth building on right. ✂ ● ⛭ ♿

FIBER NETWORK SITE
Check with EVFAC for updates about northern Fiber Arts Trails sites.

Santa Clara Trading offers a rare opportunity to see and

learn about Pueblo fiber arts – embroidered manta cloth and kilts, hand-woven sashes, belts, and hair ties, crocheted leggings, Hopi woven plaques – all part of the fabric of Pueblo ceremonial life. Knowledgeable hosts Susie Hart and Dolly Naranjo Niekrug display high quality pieces that engage the hand and mind: willow baskets, Hopi woven plaques, beadwork, ribbon and rickrack shirts, Navajo baskets and rugs, cloth, and yarn.

Memorial Day-Labor Day, M-SA, 10-5:30; SU, 12-6 Labor Day-Memorial Day, W-M, 10-5 505.747.0009 santaclaratrading.com
1.1 miles south of intersection of Hwys 84 and 30, on Hwy 30. Round building on the east side of the road, at the Thamu St. entrance to Santa Clara Pueblo.
✂ ♿ ☎

Centinela Traditional Arts

RT Davis Shepherd and Handweaver

3. BLACK MESA FIBER ARTS
South of Española
24 Pajarito Loop

Trish Spillman's studio is a delightful landscape of colors and textures. Her rag rugs, shawls, shrugs, scarves, jewelry, felted hats, and accessories are made from an array of

materials, from her own hand-dyed yarns to trimmed hems from the Santa Fe Opera's costume department, where she volunteers each year. Some of Spillman's nine looms are available for formal classes or impromptu demonstrations. And her picnic table is available to enjoy and take in a stunning view of Black Mesa.

M & TH, 10-4 505.753.3781 georgers@newmexico.com
From Española, about 8 miles south on Hwy 30. East on Avanyu Po, toward Black Mesa. Continue straight, road will become dirt. Bear left. Turn right on Pajarito Loop, over cattle guard. Studio on left, mailbox painted with sunflowers. ✂ ● ♿

4. RT DAVIS SHEPHERD AND HANDWEAVER
La Mesilla, 36 Private Drive

In a cottonwood grove along the Río Grande, a colorful flock of friendly Churro

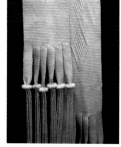
Española Valley Fiber Arts Center

sheep, their affable livestock-guarding dogs, a cat, donkeys, chickens, turkeys, and honey bees call Bob Davis's farm home. Since Davis inherited his first loom and a flock of sheep years ago, his knowledge, passion, and artistry have grown, along with his flock and collection of looms. At the farm and studio, learn about all aspects of Río Grande weaving, from raising the sheep, shearing and spinning their wool, to transforming the yarn into fine tapestries.

T & TH, 10-2 505.310.3099 riograndeweaving.com

✂ Supplies ● Classes and workshops ♿ Wheelchair accessible
♿ Wheelchair accessible restrooms ☎ Check road conditions

Española Valley Fiber Arts Center

South of Española at junction of Hwy 84/285 and 399, turn west on 399 toward La Mesilla. Right on 581. Left on CR 16. Left on CR 11 and follow to the end. Right on CR 14. Bear left on Private Drive; farm and studio are at the end of the lane. Note: Call ahead. This is a working farm, and Bob Davis wants to greet visitors at the gate. ✂

5. EARTH ARTS
La Mesilla, 7 County Road 14

At Earth Arts, experience the natural dyeing cycle in its entirety, from a garden replete with Hopi sunflowers, madder, and indigo, to stunning tapestries woven in Liesel Orend's sun-drenched studio. The walls of her dye

Earth Arts

Centinela Traditional Arts

workshop glow with a dazzling array of gem tones that she achieves through the alchemy of natural dyeing. Take home a few hanks of hand-dyed New Mexico Churro yarn or dye plant seeds for your own project, or expand your creativity in one of Orend's natural dye workshops.

T & TH, 10-2 505.753.9744
earth-arts.com
South of Española at junction of Hwy 84/285 and 399, turn west on 399 toward La Mesilla. Right on 581. Left

on CR 16. Left on CR 11 and follow to the end. Turn right on CR 14. Earth Arts is #7, on your left. ✂ 🍎 ♿

6. MARIE VIGIL WEAVINGS
Cundiyó, 1160 HWY 503
Entrada Del Arroyo

Nestled close to the Sangre de Cristo Mountains is the village of Cundiyó, where Marie Vigil continues her family's weaving tradition, using methods passed down from generations. Her work includes Chimayó and Río Grande style weaving – vests, runners, and intricate tapestries. Following her family's unique method, she uses bobbins made from wild reeds to wind her vegetal hand-dyed Churro yarn. She offers a cozy, intimate setting to view the authentic weaving process and shop for stunning, one-of-a-kind pieces.

May 1-Oct 31, F & S,
10-2 505.351.4806
North of Pojoaque on Hwy 84/285, east on SR 503. Drive 8 miles, through Nambé, past the turnoff to Chimayó. Go five more miles through the mountains to Cundiyó. Follow a winding road, cross the bridge, and turn right into Entrada del Arroyo, entering the Vigil family compound.

7. KAREN MARTINEZ STUDIO & GALLERY
Chimayó, 23B Santa Cruz Lake Road

Karen Martinez says that weaving is in her blood. It's a family tradition that has nurtured seven generations, and counting. As children, she

---

✂ Supplies 🍎 Classes and workshops ♿ Wheelchair accessible
♿ Wheelchair accessible restrooms ☎ Check road conditions

and her siblings slept in bunk beds to leave room for the walking looms tailor built for each child, and passed through the family like clothing. Today, her upstairs home studio holds 11 looms to accommodate production work, Martinez's classes, and her own creations – which favor traditional Saltillo designs and her stunning color gradations. Shop in the downstairs gallery for work ranging from placemats to collectable wall pieces, and everything in between. Check nnmc.edu, Chimayó classes, for current schedule.

All Year, SA & SU, 12-5; Mid-May–Mid-August, M & T, 8-5 505.351.1116 ecmartinez_23@hotmail.com *North of Pojoaque on Hwy 84/285, east on Rte. 503. Go 13.5 miles, past the village of Cundiyó. Just after mile marker 13, turn left on Santa Cruz Lake Road. Go 2/10 miles and enter the double black pipe gates on right. Go down dirt road to large, two-story brown stucco house with green roof, on left.* ✿

Tapetes de Lana

CARLA GOMEZ

Tapetes de Lana

WEAVING IS A CONTINUOUS THREAD in Carla Gomez's life, starting with her Spanish heritage and two grandfathers: one, a weaver from Los Luceros, and the other, a sheep rancher in Galisteo. From a childhood table loom and the spinning wheel she requested for her 18th birthday, Gomez became a weaver in her own right, selling her silk ruanas at prominent local galleries. As Curator of Textiles at the living history museum El Rancho de Las Golondrinas she deepened her personal connection to her ancestral roots. This background served her well as a Master Artist in New Mexico Arts' Folk Arts Apprenticeship Program and currently in the Arts Enterprise Partnerships program.

When she began teaching weaving for New Mexico Highlands University at her studio, a one-room school-house, she made the connection among weaving, culture, community, and livelihood, working with "real people, real life, and real issues." With a core group of dedicated students, she launched Tapetes de Lana, a nonprofit, focusing on training and marketing the work of local weavers, and developing the rural economy.

Gomez's visionary leadership and persistence have nurtured productive partnerships, continually creating new opportunities and adding value to all aspects of fiber. She says, "Throughout our country, income opportunities are becoming scarce in rural communities, as corporations move to Third World countries in search of cheap labor sources. Big corporations and big commercial farms have taken over the economy, and there's not much left in rural communities for people to advance. The work of Tapetes is really empowering, changing people's image of themselves. When they see people from all over the country, or even the world, purchasing their textiles, it gives them a lot of pride." ✱

[NORTH CENTRAL]

LEARNING LEADS TO TEACHING

BEATRICE MAESTAS SANDOVAL

From top: Española Valley Fiber Arts Center; Furniture and More.

LAS VEGAS NATIVE BEATRICE MAESTAS SANDOVAL remembers hearing about her great-grandmother, a weaver. "Somehow, I always had her in the back of my mind." When her children were grown, Sandoval dove into learning Spanish colonial traditional arts – spinning, dyeing, weaving, colcha embroidery, woodworking, and tin work. At El Rancho de Las Golondrinas, a living history museum south of Santa Fe, she learned traditional techniques for fiber arts, which she and other volunteers demonstrate for visitors in the summer. Not one for shortcuts, she spins and dyes her own yarn for weaving Río Grande rugs, as well as for the canvas, or sabanilla, on which she stitches traditional colcha embroidery. "Once you get used to your own homespun, you can't go back."

An active participant in Spanish Market, she took Best of Show in 2000 for her colcha embroidery, setting new standards that require all prizewinning colcha to be stitched on hand woven sabanilla. Her embroidery yarn is likewise her own, colored with natural dyes – indigo, cochineal, flowers, Navajo tea, even avocado pits and skins!

Sandoval has helped keep her art form alive through New Mexico Arts' Folk Arts Apprenticeship Program as a Master Artist. "They're good traditions," she said. "We need to learn from our ancestors. And we've got to teach these kids, so it won't get lost" ✳

8. CENTINELA TRADITIONAL ARTS
Chimayó, 946 State Road 76

Master weavers Lisa and Irvin Trujillo have their feet and hearts firmly planted in the Río Grande tradition. Their contemporary work takes flight in explorations of color, design, technique, and materials, making sense of the world through yarn. Weaving, family history, and community involvement resound in this studio and gallery, which carries the work of over 30 other local fiber artists: traditional and contemporary weaving, luscious chenille ruanas, classic Chimayó jackets and vests, and more. Custom orders are a specialty.

M-SA, 9-6; SU, 10-5
505.351.2180
chimayoweavers.com
North of Pojoaque on Hwy 84/285, east on Rte. 503 toward Nambé. After several miles, turn left on Rte. 98. Enter Chimayó; 98 will dead end at Rte. 76. Turn right. Drive one mile, look for a large sign on the left. ♿♿

9. LOS VIGILES LIVING TRADITIONS FIBER STUDIO & SUPPLY
Chimayó, 776 State Road 76

Under the pitched roof of this charming territorial adobe home and studio, a world of Río Grande weaving awaits. The arts: traditional hand-woven textiles in striking color combinations and natural shades from New Mexico and Colorado-raised Churro sheep. The tools: Chimayó production looms

Clockwise from left: Victory Ranch Alpacas; Koehler Studio; Viorge Designs.

designed and crafted by the Vigil family, locally made weaving, knitting, and crocheting tools for fiber artisans, and Churro yarn. The process: classes in spinning, dyeing, weaving, knitting, crocheting, and felting. Best of all, a family of passionate and knowledgeable Río Grande weavers welcomes you to their studio.

M-SA, 10-5 505.351.4522
warpweave
@cybermesa.com
From Española, 7.6 miles east on SR 76; 1/8 mile south of Rte. 98. ⚸ ● ♿ ♿

10. ORTEGA'S WEAVING SHOP

Chimayó, 53 Plaza del Cerro

Visit a studio and gallery that have been mainstays of the Río Grande weaving tradition and local economy for generations. Robert Ortega proudly carries on the family business begun by his grandfather in this family home, adjacent to Chimayó's historic Plaza del Cerro. Twenty-five weavers create rugs and blankets, as well as yardage for Ortega's signature coats, vests, and home furnishings. Classic Chimayó and Río Grande designs and high

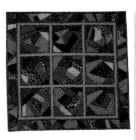

quality are longstanding hallmarks of Ortega's woven goods. Knowledgeable and congenial hosts share the weaving process and family and local history, making this stop both fun and educational.

M-SA, 9-5 877.351.4215
ortegasweaving.com
North of Pojoaque on Hwy 84/285, east on SR 503 toward Nambé. Drive several miles; left on CR 98. In Chimayó, Ortega's is on left, just before CR 98 dead ends at SR 76. ♿ ♿

11. TEJEDORAS DE LAS TRAMPAS

Las Trampas,
11 County Road 0005

In a historic farmhouse overlooking an idyllic valley, magic is taking place. The "Weavers of Las Trampas" are transforming rags into woven and crocheted rugs and baskets to brighten your home. Theirs is a gathering place for women of all ages and backgrounds to work on projects, visit with neighbors, and breathe new life into a cherished local heritage. The Tejedoras weave in their cozy studio and offer their work for sale in a two-room gallery.

TH-T, 11-5 505.689.1340
From Chimayó, go east on Hwy 76. Go 1/2 mile past mile marker 24 (Las Trampas). Left on CR 0005 for 1/10 mile. Bear right to first house and up long driveway. From Peñasco, west on Hwy 76, go 1/2 mile past mile marker 25, turn right on CR 0005. ●

[NORTH CENTRAL]

⚸ Supplies ● Classes and workshops ♿ Wheelchair accessible
♿ Wheelchair accessible restrooms ☎ Check road conditions

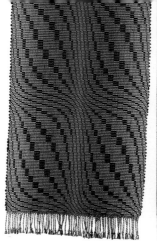

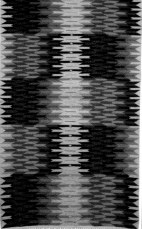

From left: Española Valley Fiber Arts Center (detail of weaving); Metier (detail of weaving).

14. SANDRASILK
Peñasco, 5 State Road 73

Step inside a world of colors and textures, a working studio where Sandra Holzman transforms silks and other fabrics into luxurious garments and home furnishings. A textile wizard, Holzman selects fabrics she paints and dyes to bring out the luster in each piece – and in the wearer. She appreciates the expression of joy on customers' faces as the sensation of silk on skin makes them feel fabulous in her creations. Special orders welcome.

May 15-Oct 15, TH & F, 12-4
505.587.2660
sandraholzman.com
From Chimayó, east on SR 76; right on SR 75 to Peñasco. Where the road curves left (north) at end of town, continue straight onto Rte. 73 toward Llano. SandraSilk is 2nd house on right.

12. METIER
Dixon, 202 SR 75

Inside this historic mercantile building in charming Dixon, you'll find high quality fiber arts, home furnishings and clothing. Owner and artist Irene Smith creates Appalachian-style baskets from reed and oak, and coiled miniatures from hand-gathered yucca, willow, and pine needles. She alternates between her four looms, weaving traditional Río Grande pieces from wool, and complex patterned wearable art in cotton, silk, rayon, and other natural fibers. Classes in basketry, weaving, spinning, and natural dyeing.

Feb 15-Dec 31, T-SU, 10-5
505.579.4111
info@metierweaving.com
From Chimayó, east on SR 76; west on SR 75, 10 miles to Dixon. Look for rock-faced building on north side. From Española, north on SR 68; east on SR 75; go 2 miles to Dixon.
🪡 ♿

13. ART FOR THE HEART
Peñasco, 14197 SR 75

A believer in the therapeutic value of art, Jean Nichols has stocked this community studio with cloth, yarns, and all manner of recyclables for creativity and play. Community members gather to work on projects, learn fiber techniques, and just visit. The gallery reflects their diversity: quilts, crochet, knitting, silk scarves, "Goddess Garb," wire sculpture, and more. Check out "Hersday," an open women's art group, Thursday afternoons, and "Glam Trash," an annual recycled fashion extravaganza!

May 1-Nov 15, TH-SU, 11-5;
Nov 16-Apr 30,
TH & SU, 11-4 & F, 1-4
505.587.0202 | 505.587.2889
art-for-the-heart.org
From Chimayó, east on SR 76; east on SR 75 to studio, on south side between mile markers 14 and 15.

Earth Arts

15. TAOS SUNFLOWER YARNS & FIBERS
Arroyo Seco,
480 State Road 150

Arroyo Seco is a little jewel of a village. A warm and inviting space in a 200-year-old adobe, Taos Sunflower overflows with handspun and dyed yarns by Taos spinners, locally dyed roving, and an abundance of commercial yarns: wools, mohair, alpaca, linen, silk, cotton, rayon, and novelty yarn. A haven for knitters, spinners, and felters, this shop carries tools, patterns, books, and more.

T-SA, 9:30-4; SU, 10:30-4
505.776.5644
taossunflower.com
North of Taos on Hwy 64. Right on Hwy 150 (road to Taos Ski Valley) for 5 miles to village of Arroyo Seco. Shop is on the left in a compound behind Doug West gallery.

From top: Santa Clara Trading;
Española Valley Fiber Arts Center.

RÍO GRANDE WEAVING
────────────

A RIBBON THROUGH TIME

Ortega's Weaving Shop

ALONG THE RÍO GRANDE RIVER VALLEY, weaving embodies a way of life planted in northern New Mexico with the first Spanish settlers, who arrived in the late 16th century with Churro sheep and the means to build treadle looms. Weaving furnished households with floor rugs, blankets, and clothing, among other utilitarian items, and, along with livestock, grew into a thriving trade in the New Mexico Territory. In the 1820s, with the opening of the Mexican border to the south and the Santa Fe Trail connecting east and west, the free flow of commerce, materials, and designs lifted Río Grande weaving to new heights. At the close of the century, the railroad came to New Mexico with its attendant tourist trade. Concurrently, the industrial revolution brought about the growth of manufactured cloth and decline in the American agrarian lifestyle. As a result, New Mexican handwoven goods were used mostly in households in more remote areas of the north and were marketed through curio shops to outsiders. The formation of locally owned businesses in weaving centers like Chimayó in the early years of the 20th century bolstered textiles as a continued livelihood and kept profits in the community.

The formation of the Spanish Colonial Arts Society in 1926 reinvigorated Río Grande weaving as an art form in its own right by promoting high quality in materials, design, and technique, and developing a market for this distinctive tradition, among other Hispanic arts. Many weavers along the Fiber Arts Trails take part in Santa Fe's annual Spanish Market, which showcases examples of an enduring tradition in its many contemporary interpretations. ✳

Weaving Southwest

16. WEAVING SOUTHWEST
Taos, 216 B Paseo del
Pueblo Norte

Devoted exclusively to
tapestry weaving, an art
form that owner Pat Dozier
describes as "weaving with
intent," Weaving Southwest
is alive with color and
features contemporary
pieces by over 18 tapestry
artists, as well as wearable
art. Get your fiber fix here
at the home of the Río
Grande Loom, the Cadillac
of looms; Río Grande
Spinning Wheel; locally
dyed Río Grande yarns; and
many other splendid yarn
varieties, tools, and books.
In the studio, weavers
specialize in filling custom
rug and blanket orders of
selected colors and designs.

M-SA, 9-5; SU, 11-4
505.758.0433
weavingsouthwest.com
*Two blocks north of Taos
Plaza, across from Kit Carson
Park in Yucca Plaza.* ✂ ●
♿ ♿

17. LA LANA WOOLS
Taos, 136 Paseo del
Pueblo Norte

An ode to naturally dyed
yarn in all its serendipity!
Luisa Gelenter and her staff
are master spinners and
dyers, creating their own
yarns – Forever Random, in
graduated blends of wool
and mohair; and Jewels and
Wild Thing, thick-spun
yarns for embellishments
and inspiration. Knitting
patterns custom-designed for
La Lana highlight their
exquisite yarns, and all can
be seen in tantalizing samples. Inquire about seasonal
knitting and needle felting
workshops and Saturday
morning knitting classes.

M-SU, 10-5:30 505.758.9631
lalanawools.com
1.5 blocks north of Taos Plaza.
✂ ●

18. RIO FERNANDO FARM
Taos, 3 Sunset Drive

In this tranquil mountain
setting, regal llamas, curious
pygora (cashmere) goats, and
fluffy angora rabbits are your
hosts. Shelley Loveless knows
her fiber, and spins and knits
beautiful blends of yarn and
her own creations. This welcoming farm offers raw fiber,
yarn, and garments for sale.
Loveless says of her furry
family's calming influence,
"You just pet them and you
relax."

Jun 1-Nov 1, T & TH,
8-12 505.758.0019
rff@laplaza.org
*From Visitors Center on Hwy
68 (Paseo del Pueblo Sur in
Taos), right onto Bypass 585
(Paseo del Cañon). When road
ends at a T, go right onto Hwy
64, east toward Angel Fire. Go
5 miles, past Shady Brook Inn.
After 7/10 mile, turn right at
cluster of mailboxes onto Sunset
Dr. Cross river; Rio Fernando
Farm is #3.* ✂ ☎

Marie Vigil Weavings

RACHEL BROWN

Background: Terrazas Traditional Arts. Above: Rachel Brown with her tapestry, left, and one by Pat Dozier, right.

TRAINED IN PAINTING and drawing when she arrived in Taos in the 1950s, Rachel Brown was inspired by her Hispanic neighbors' weaving. Her own weaving career began with reassembling an abandoned loom in a former WPA workshop and plucking stray fleece from fences for wool to spin.

Brown's *The Weaving, Spinning, and Dyeing Book*, in its 14th printing, has sold more than 100,000 copies. Brown's detailed instructions and more than 400 original drawings cover every aspect of transforming a fleece to a work of art, as well as making a living from weaving.

Brown's fiber arts experience and seemingly limitless energy were driving forces behind the creation of Tierra Wools, the weaving-based cottage industry that took root in Tierra Amarilla in 1982 and is still going strong. Her Weaving Southwest gallery in Taos has been a stronghold of high quality contemporary weaving for more than 20 years, launching the careers of many well-known New Mexico tapestry artists. Brown stocked the shelves with her own hand-dyed yarns, accomplished by refining traditional tools and processes to increase volume in addition to quality. Brown's Río Grande Loom and Río Grande Spinning Wheel are still available in the shop, which she sold to Pat Dozier in 2003.

Brown promoted weaving as an art form, hoping to nurture each weaver's design sense. "I've tried to encourage weavers to let the weaving and the medium itself dictate form. Many weavers, including myself, start out with the warp and nothing but the colors chosen, and just weave free-form like an artist goes about creating an oil painting. Weaving is more difficult because you can't go back and change anything. It's building with threads."

Brown's work creating, teaching, organizing, and marketing has forged a strong fiber arts community in New Mexico. She reflects: "I've wanted to show others the joys of weaving and that you can make a living at it. What I love most about this work is empowering people and the friendships it brings. I get passionate about teaching somebody how they can do something that will be rewarding to them." ✱

19. TAPETES DE LANA
Mora, 518 JCT 434

Tapetes de Lana – Weavings of Wool – is in a historic mercantile building transformed into a vibrant community center. In the center are a weaving studio and a gorgeous gallery of rugs, products of Tapetes de Lana students who have been trained through the nonprofit's entrepreneurial programs. Also for sale are other home furnishings woven from locally grown and processed wool; wearable arts; and an array of local yarns. Tour the mill where Tapetes processes diverse fibers into a variety of colors and textures. One-on-one weaving, spinning, and dyeing instruction available.

M-F, 8-5; SA, 10-5
Mill closed weekends; check Web site or call for tour schedules.
505.387.2247
tapetesdelana.com
From Taos, SR 518 south and east to junction with SR 434 in Mora. From Las Vegas, north on SR 518 for 30 miles to Mora.
⚒🍎♿🚻

20. VICTORY RANCH ALPACAS
Mora, 1 mile north of town on HWY 434

This 1,100-acre ranch in the majestic Mora Valley is home to 200-plus friendly alpacas. Take an informational tour with knowledgeable hosts who will walk you through every step of caring for alpacas and transforming their fleece into wonderfully soft yarn. Shearing is in June, and summer is when you just

might happen upon the birth of one of some 40 babies born at Victory Ranch each year. The Weisner family sells alpacas, alpaca yarn, alpaca garments, and high quality fiber arts. Ask about spinning and weaving classes and knitting retreats.

Feb 1-Dec 31, M-SU, 10-4; Tours at 11, 1, & 3 (fee).
505.387.2254
victoryranch.com
From Mora northeast on Hwy 434 for one mile. Ranch gate is on left. From Las Vegas, north on SR 518 for 30 miles to Mora. ⚒🍎♿🚻

21. TAPETES DE LANA
Las Vegas, 1814 Plaza

On the historic Las Vegas Plaza, enter a world of vivid colors and striking designs. With a studio and a gallery of traditional and contemporary rugs and garments, a great place to steep yourself in New Mexico's weaving heritage. Learn about spinning, dyeing, and weaving from devoted and knowledgeable artists,

From top: Metier; Santa Clara Trading; Victory Ranch Alpacas.

trained through entrepreneurial programs. One-on-one weaving, spinning, and dyeing instruction is available, and locally produced yarns tempt true fiber lovers.

⚒ Supplies 🍎 Classes and workshops ♿ Wheelchair accessible
🚻 Wheelchair accessible restrooms ☎ Check road conditions

M-F, 8-5; SA, 10-5
505.426.8638
tapetesdelana.com
*From Mora, south on SR 518
to Las Vegas. From I-25,
exit 345 (University Ave.).
Go west toward downtown.
Turn right on 7th St. Left
on National Ave. (NM 65).
Right on Gonzales St.,
which becomes Plaza Ave.
Tapetes de Lana is on northwest
corner of the plaza.*

✁ ● ♿ ⚑

22. FURNITURE AND MORE
Las Vegas, 519 Sixth Street

Three dedicated fiber artists
have transformed a corner
of a historic building in
downtown Las Vegas into
a showcase for their exquisite
work. Beatrice Maestas
Sandoval spins and dyes
her own Churro yarn that
she weaves into fine
traditional Río Grande
rugs and colcha embroidery.
Caroline Rackley weaves
tapestries, architectural
sculptures, upholstery,
domestic linens, and scarves
in rich tones and vibrant
designs. Dorothy Lake's
knitted garments are
wearable art, alive with
texture and complex
patterns. All artists display
at the annual fiber show in
Las Vegas.

M-F, 10-4 505.454.9133
505.425.8485
nmmercado.com/bmaestas
imagenm.com
*From Mora, south on SR 518
to Las Vegas. From I-25,
exit 345 (University Ave.)
west for two blocks toward
downtown. Left on Sixth St.;
go 2 blocks; shop is on right.* ♿

AN ENTREPRENEURIAL PROJECT SPONSORED
BY ESPAÑOLA VALLEY FIBER ARTS CENTER

TEJEDORAS DE LAS TRAMPAS

Tejedoras de la Trampas

BEFORE MANUFACTURED cloth became common-
place, handmade textiles were a precious commodity.
Not easily replaced, worn clothing was patched and
mended, recycled into smaller items, and finally woven
into rag rugs to salvage every thread of possible use.
Tejedoras weaving instructor Jody Ford observes that
today most used clothing ends up in the dump, wasting
good material and taking up scarce landfill space.

Tejedoras de Las Trampas, "Weaving Women of
Las Trampas," is a fiber arts cooperative that promotes
community wellness through collaborative projects
that care for the environment, bring income into local
households, ease rural isolation, and uphold cultural
heritage. Ford notes that memories are sparked at
Tejedoras. "Many people come in here and say, 'My
mother used to do this,' or 'My grandmother had the
only loom in town.'"

Tejedoras welcomes all with a desire to do handwork, learn to weave or spin, and enjoy the company
of kindred spirits, whether eight or 80 years old. The
therapeutic value of participation is clear. Says Ford,
"There's something about a sewing circle – it's just
very encompassing." ✳

A MOMENT OF PASSION

Background: Terrazas Traditional Arts. Above: Urban Eagle Herb Co. & Farm's Hopi dye sunflowers.

OUR NEW MEXICO FIBER ROOTS run deep. In the south, people have planted cotton and used its fibers for hundreds of years. Sheep have been a more adaptable fiber source since the Spanish brought them to the area. We also have natural fibers for baskets and paper at hand. New breeds of sheep, goats, rabbits, and even llamas and alpaca have been brought into New Mexico. But wool has been the predominant fiber in our artists' hands for the last 400 years. We've never ceased raising sheep, spinning their wool, dyeing it with whatever is available, and making beautiful things.

With the industrial revolution, many people quit making things with their own hands. In New Mexico, the industrial revolution brought trains and manufactured goods. Industry, per se, did not come to New Mexico: no manufacturers set up power looms here. The fiber industry was on a smaller scale. The products of people's hands were sold to visitors who wanted to bring home a piece of the exotic Southwest.

Why have fiber arts continued here in New Mexico, when they've largely been abandoned elsewhere? Because we've always had land and materials but not wealth to buy goods. Because the fiber arts have stayed economically viable in comparison to other opportunities available to us. Because if they wanted beautiful things for their homes, New Mexicans had to produce their own.

A rag rug makes good sense if you have old worn-out clothes but nothing to warm a cold floor. Willows must be cut from irrigation ditches, so why not put them to use?

Our deep fiber roots have allowed a vibrant growth in recent decades. We learn not only from generations of fiber artists who lived here before us but also from fiber traditions and innovators that have come from all over the world. Today, we have a fabulous proliferation of fiber creativity right here in New Mexico. We invite you to share our roots and our vision by visiting our fiber artists and growers. ✻

—Lisa Trujillo, Centinela Traditional Arts, and New Mexico Fiber Artisans

23. VIORGE DESIGNS
Tucumcari,
809 S Monroe Street

The fiber arts are taking off in Tucumcari, and Viorge Designs is leading the way. The Wallaces are dedicated fiber artists whose gallery showcases her pin-woven jewelry and his homespun, hand-dyed yarns that find their way into unique woven and felted garments. Beading supplies and George Wallace's handmade crochet and knitting tools and rigid heddle and triangular looms are available, along with handspun and specialty yarns. Sign up for a class or individual instruction at this working studio.

T-TH, 6-9; F, 1-9; SA, 10-6
505.461.4527 viorge.com
From Las Vegas, east on SR 104. From I-40, exit 332/First St. Go north to the first light; right on Rte. 66, also Tucumcari Blvd. East 2 blocks; right on S. Monroe. First house on the right. ⚒ ⬤

Centinela Traditional Arts

24. GOOD FIBRATIONS!
Edgewood, #4 George Court, Suite D

Bethe Orrell is doing her part to keep handwork alive and well in the East Mountains. A fiber paradise offering a huge selection of locally produced roving, yarns, and tools. A living room for knitters, a weaving area, a dye and felting kitchen, and classroom. And classes in just about every imaginable fiber art. Orrell raises sheep and angora goats, and can share information about buying or raising fiber animals. What more could you dream of? Check Web site or subscribe to e-newsletter for classes and special events.

M-SA, 10-6; T, 10-9; SU, 12-5 505.281.5963
goodfibrations.net
From I-40 east of Albuquerque, exit 187 (Edgewood). Follow signs to Rte. 66. Right at light by Smiths. Go 1/2 mile west on Old 66. Right on George Ct., into Family Dollar entrance. Shop is at the top of driveway on right. ⚒ ⬤ ♿ ♿

25. ROBIN PASCAL FIBER ARTIST & PERFECT BUTTONS
Edgewood, 58 Moriarty Road

At this fiber haven, you'll find Robin Pascal weaving, painting roving or yarn, or creating one-of-a-kind fused glass buttons in her working studio. Pascal makes her own yardage that she sews into jackets and tops. Fiber artists will revel in the selection of

From top: Victory Ranch Alpacas;
Española Valley Fiber Arts Center.

hand-painted roving (wool blends, silk, mohair, or alpaca) and hand painted yarns (cashmere, wool, silk, cotton, and rayon), kits with her yarn and patterns, and handmade buttons. Call about Saturday morning knitting classes, private weaving lessons, and one-day yarn-painting workshops.

T & W, 12-4 505.286.1783
perfect buttons.com
From I-40 east of Albuquerque, exit 187 (Edgewood). South on Hwy 344. Straight through light with Old 66, and up hill. Right onto Moriarty (a dirt road). Moriarty curves to the left, becoming Duke. Take first right onto Willard. Right onto Steeplechase at yield sign. Steeplechase ends at Moriarty Rd.; turn left. Studio is second house on the right. ⚒ ⬤ ☎

⚒ Supplies ⬤ Classes and workshops ♿ Wheelchair accessible
♿ Wheelchair accessible restrooms ☎ Check road conditions

26. SHOOTING STAR FARM
Edgewood, 12 Digby Lane

Connie Dyba's scenic fiber farm is a treat for all. Tour the farm and meet hospitable alpacas, llamas, angora goats, and sheep. Miniature donkey Itty Bitty – who stars in nativity scenes each Christmas – is a willing guide. Dyba's coloring and information sheets for young people are take-home treasures. She also has classes and individual instruction in circular knitting, tatting, lacemaking, lavender wands, and pressed flowers, plus locally made fiber arts, fiber animals, roving, fleeces, yarn, instruction and pattern books, and fiber kits for young people. Call for tours.

W-SU, 11-4 505.281.7775
shootingstar-farm.com
From I-40 east of Albuquerque, exit 181 (Sedillo). East from ramp onto Old Rte. 66. Left on Mountain Valley Rd. Right on Crestview. Right on County Line Rd. Left on Digby Lane, up hill. Farm is second driveway on right.

27. JOHNSONS OF MADRID GALLERIES OF FINE & FIBER ART
Madrid, 2843 HWY 14

The Johnsons are the "oldest newcomers" in Madrid, arriving in the '70s at the dawn of this ghost town's rebirth as an arts community. Diana and Mel Johnson's block-printed and silk-screened clothing are among the works of over 50 northern New Mexico fiber artists, whose "wearables and wallables" fill this massive space – formerly the coal truck repair garage in Madrid's coal-mining heyday. Choose from willow baskets, woven clothing, rugs, and hangings, crocheted and knitted clothing, hand-painted silks, beadwork, and much more.

Feb 1-Dec 31, M-SA, 10-6;
SU, 12-6; First SA receptions 10-6 505.471.1054
djofm@yahoo.com
From I-40, exit 175 north on SR 14 (Turquoise Trail). Across from Mineshaft Tavern. &

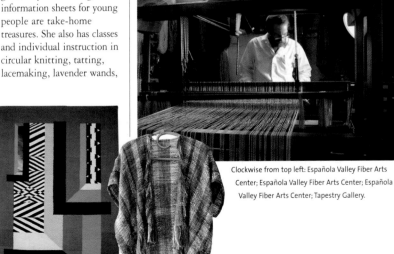

Clockwise from top left: Española Valley Fiber Arts Center; Española Valley Fiber Arts Center; Española Valley Fiber Arts Center; Tapestry Gallery.

From top: Tapetes de Lana; Española Valley Fiber Arts Center.

life in her collages. Thread-work adds color and con-tour. This working studio, with windows onto a lush arroyo, is lined with shelves of fabric, a palette of color: layers of cloth, layers of meaning.

M 1-5 & T, 9-1
505. 474.7943
laurencamp.com
From I-25, exit 271 west of Santa Fe, go west toward La Cienega on Entrada La Cienega. Left at first stop sign onto Paseo C de Baca (CR 50). Go 2/10 mile to Theresa Lane, turn left. Drive up the steep hill past barn and two houses; turn into #25. Park just past the house, and walk down hill to red stucco studio.
☎

30. KOEHLER STUDIO
Eldorado, 7 Estambre Road

James Koehler began weaving in a northern New Mexico Benedictine monastery, where the sale of liturgical vestments and home accessories of hand-dyed yarns supported the community. For years, passing the shuttle back and forth to build tapestries figured into his meditation

28. TAPESTRY GALLERY
Madrid, 04 Firehouse Lane, Suite D

An eclectic treasure trove with the work of 30 New Mexico fiber artists is tucked inside a charming adobe, where you'll find hand-woven chenille clothing, rag rugs, artist dolls, woven copper pieces, and poplar wall pockets. Expect the unexpected here. Owner Judith Colvin readily shares her knowledge about the artists, delighting in work-ing with people who are passionate about their calling: "You can feel the artists' enjoyment of their work."

Mar 16-Dec 31, M-SU, 11-5; Jan 1-Mar 15, F-M, 11-5
505.471.0194 tapgal.com
From I-40, exit 175 north on SR 14 (Turquoise Trail). In Gypsy Plaza at south end of Main. ✂

29. LAUREN CAMP FIBER ARTIST
La Cienega, 25 Theresa Lane

Lauren Camp loves sharing the stories behind her abstract and thematic figu-rative pieces, which range in size from eight inches to five feet. She paints and dyes cotton fabric, and cuts apart silk clothing, giving it a new

Lauren Camp Fiber Artist

✂ Supplies ● Classes and workshops ♿ Wheelchair accessible
♿ Wheelchair accessible restrooms ☎ Check road conditions

Clockwise from above: the High Road to Taos; Black Mesa Fiber Arts; Española Valley Fiber Arts Center.

practice, engaging him in pure creativity. Today, his bright, open studio welcomes students and visitors to learn about dyeing, design, and weaving. Koehler's world-renowned tapestries are studies of "the patterns that surround us," melding internal and external landscapes in undulating color gradations. Koehler offers individual instruction and classes; his hand-dyed yarn is for sale.

SA-T, 1-4 505.466.3924
jameskoehler.com
From I-25, exit 290 east of Santa Fe to Hwy 285; go south. Right at third entrance to Eldorado, Avenida Eldorado. Go 7/10 mile. Right on Avenida Compadres. Left on Herrada. Third right, Estambre Rd. Studio is second drive on left. ✂ ● ♿

31. SEEDSHAMAN
Glorieta,
39 Velasquez Road

Twenty-plus years ago, Richard Solomon, then a marketing consultant for the World Wildlife Fund in Manhattan, was walking in the country when he encountered a stand of grass whose beauty stopped him in his tracks. He wondered: "How can I make my way in the world using this beauty?" Today, Solomon sculpts with plant materials, which are tied and wrapped with yucca fibers. His flat pieces suspend layers of seeds in Plexiglass as if floating in space to form breathtaking designs. Nature's magnificence abounds in and outside of his working studio in the forest.

TH-SA, 10-3 505.757.2855
seedshaman.com
From I-25, exit 299 east of Santa Fe. Go north from ramp, then right at the T, onto SR50. Continue two streets past 3-mile marker. Left on Velasquez; 4/10 mile on dirt road; left into #39. ☎

STRETCHING THE BOUNDARIES

CONTEMPORARY FIBER ARTS stretch the boundaries, challenging the senses with ever-expanding possibilities. In the fertile soil of venerable fiber traditions, New Mexico contemporary fiber arts have taken root, as generations of artists have found home in a place where reverence for daring creativity reigns.

Traditional arts themselves remain vibrant through innovation. At Centinela Traditional Arts, Lisa and Irvin Trujillo are forging new ground within the Río Grande weaving tradition, through ongoing explorations beyond the canon.

Where does inspiration live? Internationally acclaimed tapestry artist James Koehler finds patterns in nature, in chaos theory, and spiritual connections. From his background in chemistry comes a growing palette of dyes, producing the color gradations that give his work depth.

Sculptor Julie Wagner and Seedshaman Richard Solomon incorporate natural materials directly into their pieces, celebrating fiber's innate forms.

Holly Modine combines her background as a 3-D artist with her love of the tactile art of basketry. Scrap metal, bolts, and wires find their way into her sculptural baskets, along with natural materials.

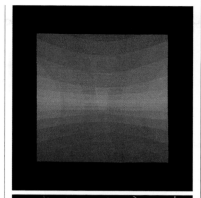

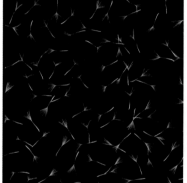

Background: Terrazas Traditional Arts. From top: Koehler Studio; Seedshaman. Left: Julie Wagner Studio.

Contemporary fiber artists Ramona Sakiestewa and Lauren Camp make collages that combine their own art work, which they cut up or "deconstruct,"

with magazine clippings, as the basis for new pieces. In the process, they are reconfiguring color, form, and texture to create something fresh, embodying the very essence of contemporary work.

Many contemporary fiber artists work in series, delving into permutations of an idea until it runs its course. The operative principle for all is exploration, whether it be of new technique, materials, designs, or avenues for personal expression. Most often, these elements work in tandem and are inseparable. ✳

Many weavers say they start out with an idea, but the design takes off
on its own. It's a collaboration between the weaver and the design.
The design is a gift. It is visualized, not drawn. As you go along,
it develops in a cycle of moving forward with life.

—YIN-MAY LEE
RAMAH NAVAJO WEAVERS ASSOCIATION

NORTHWEST LOOP

Some of New Mexico's earliest history is written in fiber. Across centuries, our dry climate has been kind, leaving yucca sandals, cotton blankets, and baskets to behold and ponder. All speak of deft fingers that gathered materials from the land and crafted things of beauty, for practical use, for ceremonial practice, for the joy of creation.

Pueblo, Navajo, and Spanish colonial textiles are strands in a braid inextricably woven with history, culture, environment, trade, and tourism — complex relationships of mutual influence. New migrations of artists overlay inspiration and energy onto this unique and treasured landscape. Artifacts endure through time. But it's the process and passion, connection between land and community, that buoy fiber art forms, threads from the past, ever with a new twist.

In northwest New Mexico, beauty wells up in red rock symphonies, in vast stretches of open space and sacred geology, in deep pine forests and volcanic plains, sparkling rivers, grassy meadows, and majestic mountains.

Creativity lives in tucked-away studios, where welcoming artists share timeless techniques and contemporary interpretations – and from where they sit, stunning views, gemlike gardens, and deep knowledge of place. Across an interconnected web, weavers gather to breathe new life into local traditions, create a good living at home, and enjoy the company of kindred spirits. Dyers conjure color from the earth. Trading posts maintain the custom of cultural and artistic exchange. Museums hold treasures past and present, in landscapes of endless fascination. Step into these worlds and experience creativity at its source. ✳

Background: Shiprock Peak. Inset: Shiprock Trading Post.

[NORTHWEST]

43 Upper Fruitland

Shiprock

42 Chama

64

41 Los Ojos

64

84

44 **FARMINGTON**

491

40 Ghost Ranch

32–34
El Rito

45 Toadlena

96

554

39 Youngsville

19

35–38
Abiquiú

46 Two Grey Hills

Chi

491

Españ

SANTA

29 La Cienega

Gallup

I-25

I-40

14

66

24–2(

602

ALBUQUERQUE

53

Grants

I-40

125

53

Los Lunas

47 Pine Hill

47

48 Tomé

Belen

47

I-25

53 Datil

60

Magdalena
49–52

Socorro

I-25

380

Rio Grande

54 Chloride

52

Map not to scale; includes trail routes only. Consult your detailed New Mexico State Map.

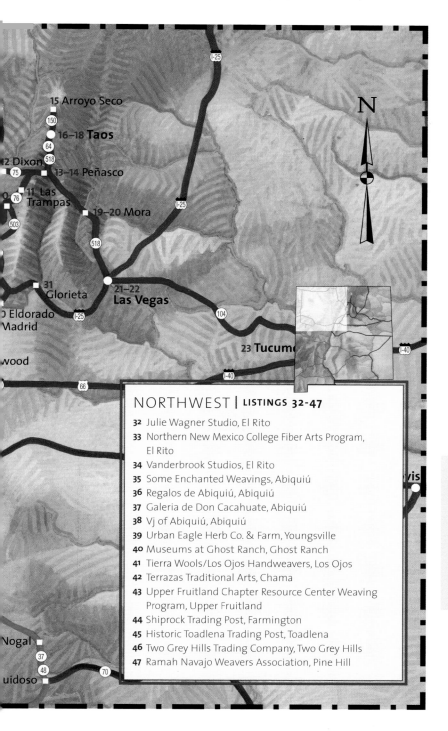

N

15 Arroyo Seco

150

16–18 Taos

64

2 Dixon 518

75

13–14 Peñasco

76

11 Las
Trampas

503

19–20 Mora

518

31
Glorieta

21–22
Las Vegas

Eldorado I-25
Madrid

104

wood

23 **Tucum**

I-40

66

I-40

Nogal

37

48

70

uidoso

NORTHWEST | LISTINGS 32-47

32 Julie Wagner Studio, El Rito
33 Northern New Mexico College Fiber Arts Program, El Rito
34 Vanderbrook Studios, El Rito
35 Some Enchanted Weavings, Abiquiú
36 Regalos de Abiquiú, Abiquiú
37 Galeria de Don Cacahuate, Abiquiú
38 Vj of Abiquiú, Abiquiú
39 Urban Eagle Herb Co. & Farm, Youngsville
40 Museums at Ghost Ranch, Ghost Ranch
41 Tierra Wools/Los Ojos Handweavers, Los Ojos
42 Terrazas Traditional Arts, Chama
43 Upper Fruitland Chapter Resource Center Weaving Program, Upper Fruitland
44 Shiprock Trading Post, Farmington
45 Historic Toadlena Trading Post, Toadlena
46 Two Grey Hills Trading Company, Two Grey Hills
47 Ramah Navajo Weavers Association, Pine Hill

vis

[NORTHWEST]

From top: Historic Toadlena Trading Post; Some Enchanted Weavings; Terrazas Traditional Arts.

A spacious dye kitchen and a spinning studio. Best of all is the blend of enduring tradition, experimentation, and innovation, and exchange as students and teachers engage as a learning community.

Mid-Aug–Mid-May,
M-TH, 8:30-2:30
505.581.4113 nnmc.edu
Note: Check Web site for current schedule.
*North of Española on Hwy 84.
Just after the 208 mile marker,
turn east on Hwy 554 toward
El Rito. Left through stone
gate onto the NNMC campus.
Bear right around circle, past
Electricity and Automotive
buildings. Fiber Arts
Building is on your right.*
✄ ● ⛾ ♿

32. JULIE WAGNER STUDIO
El Rito, County Road 231, House #21

At Julie Wagner's 100-year-old adobe, it's hard to tell where nature leaves off and the studio begins. With sweeping vistas of the Sangre de Cristo mountains, this working space is a delightful haven for Wagner's fiber sculptures, handmade books, and works on paper. Wagner remembers childhood days spent roaming the woods and bringing home leaves, bugs, and rocks – firsthand teachers about nature's life cycles. Today, she gathers many materials from the landscape that end up in her artwork.

Apr-Nov T & W, 11-5
505.581.4780
micky_julu@espanola-nm.com
*North of Española on Hwy 84.
Just after the 208 mile marker,
turn east on Hwy 554 toward
El Rito. Go 11 miles and turn
right on CR 571. Go 3/10
mile and turn left on
CR 231. Studio is first house
on the left, #21.*

33. NORTHERN NEW MEXICO COLLEGE FIBER ARTS PROGRAM
El Rito, HWY 554

Experience every phase of Río Grande weaving, from fleece to finished textile. A loom-filled room where students' and teachers' weavings adorn the walls. The resounding thunk-thunk of rows being tamped into place, a heartbeat of wood and yarn. Rooms brimming with naturally dyed yarn in a breathtaking palette of hues.

34. VANDERBROOK STUDIOS
El Rito, #02 County Road 246

Kathleen Vanderbrook mixes media to create a remarkable array of pieces that variously combine quilting, handmade paper, painting and printing, to take you on a journey of textures. Her artwork fuses materials and ideas from the natural world and interweaves community in enchanting ways. Knowing her passion for recycling and experimentation, neighbors have saved such items as corduroy scraps, library catalog cards, dryer lint, and special grasses from horse pastures for her to work into her art.

Apr-Sep, SA-W, 12-5;
Oct-Mar, SA & SU, 12-4
505.581.4597

✄ Supplies ● Classes and workshops ⛾ Wheelchair accessible
♿ Wheelchair accessible restrooms ☎ Check road conditions

North of Española on Hwy 84.
Just after the 208 mile marker,
turn east on Hwy 554 toward
El Rito. After mile marker 11,
left on CR 246. Studios sign
on Rte. 554 at junction of
CR 246.

35. SOME ENCHANTED WEAVINGS

Abiquiú, County Road
1622, House #24

Ann Lumaghi built her own
adobe home along the
Chama River and surround-
ed it with gardens. It's her
own paradise. Her studio
looks upon this natural
splendor while inside her five
looms are always busy. Rag
rugs are her specialty –
woven from cloth, beach
towels, or Pendleton blanket
selvages. She also makes
shawls, scarves, and placemats from crisp, colorful silk,
cotton, and rayon. Design
your own piece – Lumaghi
welcomes custom orders.

M-F, 1-4 505.685.4503
annlumaghi@
cybermesa.com
*From Española, north on Hwy
84 to Abiquiú. Just past mile
marker 210, turn east onto
CR 1622, then left over cattle
guard, and down a long dirt
road. House #24 is on right.*

Galeria de Don Cacahuate

NAVAJO/DINÉ WEAVING

SONG OF RESILIENCE

Historic Toadlena Trading Post

NAVAJO WEAVING IS A SONG OF RESILIENCE,
carrying the People's story through time in threads of
continuity and change. Once, all Navajo weavers spun
naturally colored yarn from the wool of their flocks.
Stripes, blocks, diamonds, and triangles created patterns
that draped the body. With increased interaction with
European cultures, velvet and calico became the fashion.
Some weavers embraced factory-made yarns and commercial dyes, gaining more time for designing and
weaving. Saltillo patterns inspired by Hispanic weaving,
pictorial interpretations of their changing world, and
regional rug designs promoted by reservation traders
for the outside market contributed to an explosion
of new designs in Navajo weaving around the turn of
the 19th century.

What hasn't changed is the ingenious simplicity
of the upright Navajo loom. Another constant is the
balance of family and cultural tradition with personal
innovation each weaver brings to her work. Weavers
today have an unprecedented abundance of choices
in materials, designs, and markets, thanks to paved
roads and publicity. Like any tradition, Navajo weaving
is a cross-fertilization of time, place, and individuality.
Regardless of individual variation, most weavers find
in their work a meditative refuge from daily cares, a
cherished vehicle of self-expression, cultural and
individual identity, and a means of income. ✳

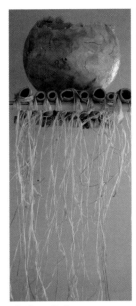

Julie Wagner Studio

36. REGALOS DE ABIQUIÚ
Abiquiú, Mile Marker 212
HWY 84

A gem within a gem within a gem is in the heart of Abiquiú's commercial district. Inside Bode's General Merchandise, you'll find Regalos de Abiquiú gallery, a treasure chest of fiber arts that speak to northern New Mexico's unique heritage:

Navajo rugs, Río Grande weaving, and all manner of traditional and contemporary handwork – quilting, beadwork, embroidery, knitting, crochet, lacework, fiber sculpture and more. Ask the staff about the art forms, the artists, and the area.

Apr 1-Dec 31, M-SU, 10-5;
Jan 1-Mar 31, TH-M, 10-5
505.685.4948
regalosnm.com
On Hwy 84 in Abiquiú, inside Bode's General Merchandise.
&. &.

37. GALERIA DE DON CACAHUATE
Abiquiú, Private Drive 1625 #8

In an old adobe that has been home to co-owner Leopoldo Garcia's family for five generations, business partner Barbara Manzanares keeps a loom and showcases her wall hangings, blankets, runners, and more. From her Navajo and Spanish roots, she weaves her cultural and family heritage into richly colored pieces from her own hand-dyed yarns. The hues of the land come alive in her work. In spring, summer, and fall, Manzanares offers natural dye workshops. She

Shiprock Trading Post

and Garcia are well versed in local history, which they gladly share with visitors.

Apr-Oct, T-SU, 9-5; Nov 1-Mar 30, TH-M, 10-5
505.685.0568
From Hwy 84 in Abiquiú, across from Bode's General Merchandise, turn up hill into old Abiquiú village. South of St. Thomas Church, Private Drive 1625 is on left. ✂ ●

38. VJ OF ABIQUIÚ
Abiquiú, County Road 189 Lane 1633, Gate 20

Vj Montanye comes by her fiber talents naturally, from a grandmother who quilted and great aunts who beaded moccasins. Montanye's contemporary work springs from these traditions. The landscape and cultures around her inspire wall quilts, stories pieced from cotton embellished with silk, thread, beads, and yarn. Her striking neckwear incorporates her own beadwork and handmade beads by others. Individual and group classes are available in beading and beginning quilting.

SA & SU, 12-4
505.685.4617

The road to Two Grey Hills Trading Post

✂ Supplies ● Classes and workshops &. Wheelchair accessible
&. Wheelchair accessible restrooms ☎ Check road conditions

From Española, north on Hwy 84 to Abiquiú. Just past Bode's General Merchandise, south on CR 189. Continue on winding road. Right on Lane #1633 through Gate #20. Drive to top of mesa on dirt and gravel road. Studio is at end of house.

🍎 ☎

39. **URBAN EAGLE HERB CO. & FARM**
Youngsville, 3698 HWY 96

At this welcoming farm, Katy Blanchard spins local fleece into yarn, which she dyes in vibrant colors from her garden. Her sweaters, vests, and hats are inspired by Native American designs. Learn about Puebloan waffle gardening techniques, and cultivation, care, and use of traditional dye plants. In season, when available, take home seeds or plants for your dye garden from hers. Ask Blanchard about her Herbal Moth-Away blend.

Jul & Aug, F & SA, 8-12
505.638.0306
urbaneagle.com
From Española, Hwy 84 north past Abiquiú. West on Rte. 96, (to Abiquiú Lake). Drive 11 miles, through Youngsville to mile marker 37. Turn left at the end of the guard rails. Cross a cattle guard, bear left, and go through the green pipe gate. Garden is on your right.
✂

Urban Eagle Herb Co. & Farm entrance

THE LANGUAGE OF DESIGN

RAMONA SAKIESTEWA
[2006 GOVERNOR'S AWARD FOR EXCELLENCE IN THE ARTS]

"Eclipse 1," wool tapestry by Ramona Sakiestewa.

RAMONA SAKIESTEWA GREW UP IN Albuquerque at a time when people sewed their own clothing and darned socks. Connecting to her Hopi roots, she taught herself all aspects of pre-historic and historical Southwest fiber arts, from spinning to dyeing to weaving. This thorough understanding has been a bridge to her contemporary tapestries, and her explorations of texture, vibrant color, and layered geometric shapes. Much of her work today centers on design, as she collaborates with architects to enhance buildings with details. Her participation in the design of the National Museum of the American Indian in Washington, DC, was a study of fiber writ large: a woven copper wall, the rim of a basket emerging from the earth, an homage to the indigenous people of that area.

Sakiestewa respects early fiber artists for their impressive and labor-intensive work. Early cloth speaks to her of connection: "It's an amazing document. There's so much encoded in the fabric itself. You've got the individual artist, where and how it was manufactured, what the plants and the dyes might have been, the reason for making it. It's like a woven 'chip' of history. Living, breathing people somehow participated in its creation."

Sakiestewa hopes that by guiding visitors to those who still engage in these processes, the Fiber Arts Trails will bring others to share her reverence for New Mexico fiber arts and help to restore the value of handmade items. ✳

[NORTHWEST]

GROWING LIVELIHOOD AT HOME

SUSTAINABILITY IN THREE STRANDS

Tierra Wools/Los Ojos Handweavers

A VITAL THREAD IN NEW MEXICO'S CULTURAL, artistic, and economic landscape, the fiber arts are a natural for rural economic development. Three sites on the Fiber Arts Trails are models for what can be accomplished when talented and dedicated citizens work together to revitalize cultural traditions that generate rural income.

The Ramah Navajo Weavers Association was the first cooperative of its kind to enhance land-based livelihoods through a focus on traditional weaving. For more than 20 years, the Ramah weavers have worked through a community process aimed at rebuilding Churro flocks, encouraging fine spinning, expanding natural dye colors, and setting high standards for weaving.

Through a series of partnerships, Tapetes de Lana has evolved from a Welfare-to-Work program to a rural economic development initiative. Today, it's flourishing with two sites – a downtown gallery and workshop in Las Vegas, and a weaving studio, gallery, conference room, and 11,000-square-foot mill in Mora.

Tierra Wools was founded as a nonprofit over 20 years ago to revive local heritage and create opportunities for weavers to earn income. It's now a thriving locally owned and operated for profit, with classes in spinning, dyeing, and weaving that keep the art forms alive while drawing visitors to its beautiful setting.

Despite diverse cultures and histories, these sites share common principles for sustainability. They've been built by grassroots efforts that reflect community needs and value the area's heritage. And they have the flexibility to grow and change with the times, as new ideas evolve. ✱

40. MUSEUMS AT GHOST RANCH
North of Abiquiú,
Mile Marker 224 HWY 84

New Mexico's interwoven heritage comes alive at the Florence Hawley Ellis Museum of Anthropology. Rotating exhibits featuring the work of regional fiber arts guilds and Northern New Mexico College students cycle through the calendar, sharing space on thick adobe walls with the museum's permanent collection of prehistoric, historical, and contemporary Native American and Spanish colonial arts. The exhibits offer a diversity of locally produced traditional and contemporary arts: weaving, embroidery, beadwork, knitting, crocheting, hand-dyed yarn, and basketry. Classes in fiber arts are available year round.

All Year, T-SA, 9-5;
Memorial Day-Labor Day,
SU, 1-5; Closed last two
weeks of Dec
505.685.4333 x118
ghostranch.org
From Española, take Hwy 84 north toward Chama. After mile marker 224, 14 miles north of Abiquiú, enter Ghost Ranch Education and Retreat Center on right. Follow an accessible gravel road and bear left to arrive at the museum. ● ♿ ♿

Vj of Abiquiú

41. TIERRA WOOLS/LOS OJOS HANDWEAVERS
Los Ojos, 91 Main St

Adobe, wood, and stone – feel the warmth of this historic mercantile building filled with brilliant color and design. Wander through galleries vibrant with Río Grande blankets and rugs, and a great selection of fiber arts made by local artisans. Demonstration and production looms and a busy dyeing area invite customers to learn about spinning, dyeing, and weaving firsthand. Take a class, or shop for locally produced yarn, knitting and weaving tools, or books.

Jun-Oct, M-SA, 9-6; SU, 11-4; Nov-May, M-SA, 10-5
505.588.7231
handweavers.com
North on Hwy 84. From intersection of Hwy 84 and Hwy 64 at mile marker 175, go 2.3 miles north to Hwy 112 and turn left. Take immediate right onto Hwy 514. Go 8/10 mile into village of Los Ojos. Tierra Wools is on your left. ✂️ 🍎 ♿ ♿

From top: Urban Eagle Herb Co. & Farm; Regalos de Abiquiú; Some Enchanted Weavings; Northern New Mexico College Fiber Arts Program .

42. TERRAZAS TRADITIONAL ARTS
Chama, 16288 HWY 84

In this working studio, you will see all phases of traditional Río Grande weaving, from skirting and washing local wool, to spinning and natural dyeing, to weaving intricately patterned blankets. Johanna Terrazas lovingly tends to each step, to ensure the high quality of her work. She has researched and revived the wedding blanket, customarily woven as a gift that joined two families in the Spanish colonial Río Grande tradition.

M & T, 9-5 505.756.2907
ltu.llc@valornet.com
On Hwy 84, 1.5 miles south of Chama and 10 miles north of Los Ojos. Just north of mile marker 163, near historic marker.
♿ ♿

43. UPPER FRUITLAND CHAPTER RESOURCE CENTER WEAVING PROGRAM
Upper Fruitland

At the Weaving Program, you'll meet a dedicated group of Navajo weavers of all ages. The common thread is a passion for learning and teaching every phase of the weaving process: carding, washing, spinning, dyeing wool, weaving on upright looms, lap looms, and sash-belt looms. Pull up a chair to learn firsthand about Navajo weaving, or try your own hand at one of these techniques.

Oct 1-May 31
TH & F, 1:30-6:30
505.598.9478
Note: Call ahead to arrange for demonstrations in spinning, dyeing, or weaving techniques.

✂️ Supplies 🍎 Classes and workshops ♿ Wheelchair accessible
♿ Wheelchair accessible restrooms ☎ Check road conditions

[NORTHWEST]

DESIGNING A LIFE OF BEAUTY

CLARA SHERMAN

[2006 GOVERNOR'S AWARD FOR EXCELLENCE IN THE ARTS]

Background: Terrazas Traditional Arts. Above: Clara Sherman with one of her rugs. Look for Sherman's weavings at Historic Toadlena Trading Post.

WHEN SHE WAS LITTLE Clara Sherman and her sister gathered wool for spinning by chasing the family flock through a fence, where tufts of fleece caught on the wires. Their mother was unwilling to squander her good homespun yarn on novice weavers. She also taught her daughters to keep their knowledge of farming, caring for sheep, and weaving to themselves, so that each would learn independently, sharpening her own mind.

Sherman's Churro sheep are descendants of her mother's flock. They run in the arroyos near her home, and in the evenings she rattles a can filled with dried corn, calling them home, *"Behe, behe, behe."* Sherman, who was born to the Hashtł'ishnii (Mud) Clan and for the Naashashi (Bear) Clan, thinks of her sheep as both her children and her parents, a relationship of mutual caring and dependency.

Her colorful flock is the palette for Sherman's exquisite tapestries, woven from her own fine homespun yarn. When she begins a rug, she envisions the design in her mind. She describes the design process as a series of "footprints" or motifs, repeating in patterns across the rug.

For Sherman, weaving is a friend that has supported her all her life. To her, weaving is a glass window through which she sees the brightness of her life, past and future. Each rug holds vivid memories, a chapter unfolding over the year or more it takes to make it. When she takes a rug off the loom, she feels an initial sadness at seeing it go, with all her thoughts woven into its design. Ultimately, she lets it go to make room in her mind for the next rug. "It's like everyday life and Mother Earth. Each year, new crops grow, new lambs are born. Things come and go." ✳

Approaching Farmington from the east, on NM 64 W, take 64 Truck Bypass. Left on Hwy 371, also Bisti Hwy, at the traffic light. Right on Navajo Rte. 36, also Upper Fruitland Hwy, and travel 5.5 miles. Go left, following the sign for Upper Fruitland. Upper Fruitland Chapter Resource Center is on left. ✄🍎♿

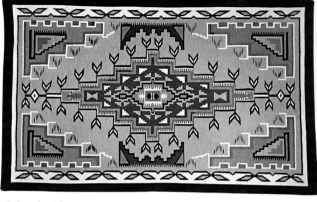

Clockwise from left: Upper Fruitland Chapter Resource Center Weaving Program; Historic Toadlena Trading Post; Museums at Ghost Ranch.

44. SHIPROCK TRADING POST
Farmington,
301 W Main Street

Fifth-generation trader Jed Foutz has seen many changes in the trading business over the years. Good rapport with local Navajo artists and work of the highest quality are threads of continuity. Foutz and his knowledgeable staff estimate that their Rolodex of local weavers holds around 1,000 names. The rug room at Shiprock Trading offers dazzling proof of this abundance in its range of regional designs and individual styles of contemporary Navajo weaving. Yarn, weaving tools, and a selection of books about Navajo arts and culture are also available. ✄♿

M-F, 9-6; SA, 9-2
505.324.0881
800.210.7847 (rugs)
shiprocktrading.com

45. HISTORIC TOADLENA TRADING POST
Toadlena, HWY N 19

Step inside the original 1909 Toadlena Trading Post building and you'll be in the "bullpen," a hallmark of early trading post days. Trader Mark Winter's Two Grey Hills Museum is a rotating display of fine spinning and weaving, past and present. In summer, buy an ice cream from the cooler and take in the view of the two grey hills from the porch. In winter, sit in the old barber's chair by the woodstove. Contemporary and historical rugs are for sale in the historic trader's quarters.

Apr 1-Dec 30, M-SU, 9-6;
Dec 31-Mar 30, M-SA, 9-5
505.789.3267
toadlenatradingpost.com
From Shiprock, south on Hwy 491; west on N19 for 10 miles. ✄

✄ Supplies 🍎 Classes and workshops ♿ Wheelchair accessible
♿ Wheelchair accessible restrooms ☎ Check road conditions

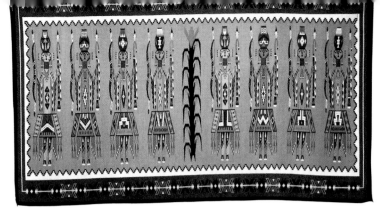

46. TWO GREY HILLS TRADING COMPANY
Two Grey Hills, Jct 5000 & N 5001

Visit the trading post that put the venerable Two Grey Hills Navajo rug design on the map. Local weavers take pride in finely spinning their own Churro wool and weaving intricate designs from a palette of natural browns, greys, ivory, and black – the colors of their flocks. Trader Les Wilson is the ninth owner of this post, which opened in 1897. The rug room showcases weaving by artists of all ages. See Wilson's album of historical photos and documents for a fascinating journey back in time. Locally produced wool and weaving tools available.

M-SA, 8:30-5 505.789.3270
twogreyhills.com

From top: Shiprock Trading Post (detail); Upper Fruitland Chapter Resource Center Weaving Program; Historic Toadlena Trading Post; Vanderbrook Studios.

From Shiprock, south on Hwy 491, west on N19 for 7 miles; south on N5000 for 3 miles. Follow signs. ✄

47. RAMAH NAVAJO WEAVERS ASSOCIATION
Pine Hill, BIA Route 125

In the heart of ponderosa pine country, in the Ramah Navajo community, the Ramah Navajo Weavers Association welcomes you to their hogan, a traditional eight-sided Navajo dwelling. These weavers maintain their own standards for beautiful rugs and pillows. All are woven with locally grown, handspun, naturally dyed Churro wool. High quality weaving and original designs are their hallmark. Learn firsthand about traditional Navajo wool preparation, handspinning, and weaving, time-honored processes for the expression of individual creativity and Diné identity.

May 1-Nov 30, TH, 12-4 & F, 10-2 505.775.3254
bobh@phwarriors.cc
From Gallup, south on SR 602 for 29 miles. East on SR 53 about 20 miles. Turn south onto BIA Rte. 125. Go 12 miles to Pine Hill. Turn left to Ramah Navajo School Board, Inc. complex. Take first right at first road to the RNWA hogan. ♿

✄ Supplies ● Classes and workshops ♿ Wheelchair accessible
♿ Wheelchair accessible restrooms ☎ Check road conditions

TRADING POSTS AND NAVAJO WEAVING

A CULTURAL EXCHANGE

Background: Terrazas Traditional Arts. Above: Historic Toadlena Trading Post.

FOR CENTURIES, NAVAJO OR DINÉ weaving has been treasured in the Southwest trade network for its beauty and quality. With the establishment of the Navajo Reservation in 1868, trading posts became the hub of Navajo life, a meeting place for far-flung communities, serving as mercantile, bank, post office, and more. Many trading posts had guest hogans – traditional Navajo dwellings – welcoming visitors to linger for hours or days. Navajo customers brought livestock, wool, piñon, and traditional arts to exchange for dry goods, food, enamel cookware, and other staples.

During the latter years of the 19th century, increased European settlement and the advent of the railroad and tourism to the Southwest forged a market for Native American arts. A downturn in the wool trade inspired traders to promote weaving as a better return on the Navajo wool harvest. Tapping popular taste for oriental carpets, traders encouraged weavers to make thicker pieces that could serve as floor rugs. As the link between weavers and the outside market, traders embraced diverse notions of taste. Regional rug designs named for particular trading posts emerged at this juncture and are still current today.

In the mid-20th century, a cash economy gradually replaced the traditional barter system as Navajo people increasingly left the reservation for wage work, boarding school, and military service, and as paved roads and pickup trucks facilitated travel. Today, Navajo weavers still contribute to their families' livelihood but generally sell their rugs for cash.

"Trading post" now encompasses anything and everything from convenience stores to high-end galleries. Shiprock Trading Post exemplifies the latter, while posts like Two Grey Hills and Toadlena, once the norm, are among the handful of trading posts where you can still buy a can of soup or a bottle of shampoo, check out the community bulletin board, or buy a handwoven Navajo rug of the highest quality. ✳

When you feel like the world is out of control, it is comforting to do something that is so traditional and grounding. They're sending people to the moon, but when I weave, I'm still doing the same thing people did thousands of years ago.

—CHARMEINE WAIT
THE COMMON THREAD

SOUTHERN LOOP

Thread your way south along the Río Grande, accompanied on its route by majestic cottonwood bosques and villages settled like pearls on a string. The land opens into the Chihuahuan desert, with sage giving way to creosote, mesquite, towering yucca sentinels, stands of prickly pear, graceful ocotillo, and carpets of wildflowers in the spring, a vibrant tapestry of random colors.

Drift off the I-25 corridor through wildly diverse, breathtaking vistas to discover hidden gems. Where once silver drew settlers to boom and bust towns, today's residents count their fortune in dwelling in close-knit communities, with natural beauty and quiet as their treasure.

Throughout this landscape of contrasts, you'll never leave sight of mountains – some rising distantly in sculptural splendor, others embracing you closely in their piney folds. In Hatch and parts south, New Mexico chile radiates in rows from the river, amid cotton fields and enchanted pistachio and pecan groves.

It's all about passion, the desire to sit in quiet meditation on color and design, growing from the connection between knowing fingers and focused mind. Yet, handworkers crave community, gathering together to stretch creativity, earn a livelihood from their hands, and share in life's unfolding stories.

Here you know there's strength in numbers. In fiber-based organizations and programs, in cooperative and group galleries, in fiber businesses – everyone is of value to the larger whole. Spectacular scenery, welcoming artists eager to share their extraordinary fiber creations, and an open invitation to participate. What more could you desire? ✳

Background: The road between Deming and Silver City. Inset: Tomé Art Gallery straw appliqué.

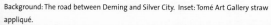

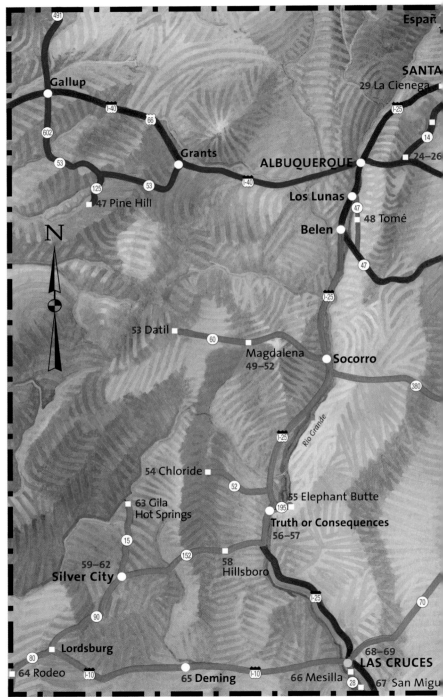

Españ

SANTA

29 La Cienega

I-25

14

24–26

Gallup

I-40

66

602

53

125

47 Pine Hill

Grants

53

53

ALBUQUERQUE

I-40

Los Lunas

47

48 Tomé

Belen

47

I-25

N

53 Datil

60

Magdalena
49–52

Socorro

380

I-25

Rio Grande

54 Chloride

52

55 Elephant Butte

63 Gila
Hot Springs

195

Truth or Consequences
56–57

15

59–62

152

58
Hillsboro

Silver City

I-25

70

90

68–69

Lordsburg

LAS CRUCES

80

64 Rodeo

I-10

65 Deming

I-10

66 Mesilla

28

67 San Migu

Map not to scale; includes trail routes only. Consult your detailed New Mexico State Map.

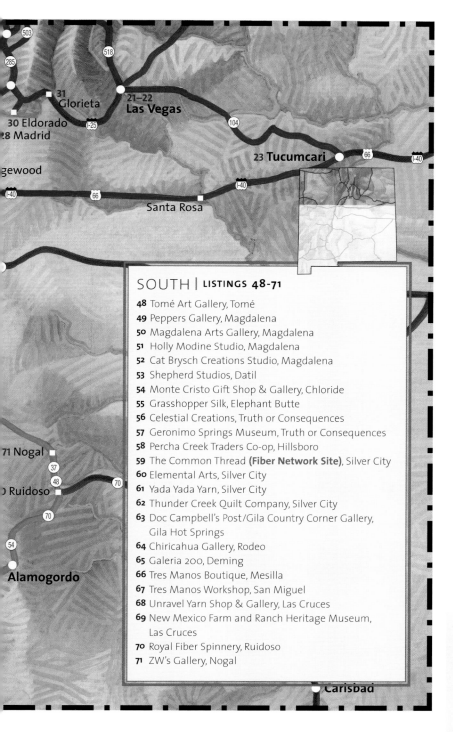

503

285

518

31
Glorieta

21–22
Las Vegas

104

30 Eldorado
28 Madrid

I-25

23 **Tucumcari**

66

I-40

gewood

I-40

66

66

I-40

Santa Rosa

SOUTH | LISTINGS 48-71

48 Tomé Art Gallery, Tomé
49 Peppers Gallery, Magdalena
50 Magdalena Arts Gallery, Magdalena
51 Holly Modine Studio, Magdalena
52 Cat Brysch Creations Studio, Magdalena
53 Shepherd Studios, Datil
54 Monte Cristo Gift Shop & Gallery, Chloride
55 Grasshopper Silk, Elephant Butte
56 Celestial Creations, Truth or Consequences
57 Geronimo Springs Museum, Truth or Consequences
58 Percha Creek Traders Co-op, Hillsboro
59 The Common Thread **(Fiber Network Site)**, Silver City
60 Elemental Arts, Silver City
61 Yada Yada Yarn, Silver City
62 Thunder Creek Quilt Company, Silver City
63 Doc Campbell's Post/Gila Country Corner Gallery,
   Gila Hot Springs
64 Chiricahua Gallery, Rodeo
65 Galeria 200, Deming
66 Tres Manos Boutique, Mesilla
67 Tres Manos Workshop, San Miguel
68 Unravel Yarn Shop & Gallery, Las Cruces
69 New Mexico Farm and Ranch Heritage Museum,
   Las Cruces
70 Royal Fiber Spinnery, Ruidoso
71 ZW's Gallery, Nogal

71 Nogal

37

48

70

Ruidoso

70

54

Alamogordo

Carlsbad

[SOUTH]

BETTY REYNOLDS

Background: Earth Arts. Inset: Percha Creek Traders Co-op.

BETTY REYNOLDS' QUILTS MELD traditional quilt blocks with contemporary materials: batiks and watercolor prints glowing with color. The old patterns stand the test of time but are amenable to innovation. She collects fabric wherever she travels, and her expertise as a former librarian leads her to sources on the Web.

Reynolds sells her work and enjoys contributing to charity quilting projects. But some of her quilts are keepers. When she first retired from her 18-year directorship at the New Mexico Tech Library in Socorro, she spent hours each day conversing with other quilters online. Swaps with her virtual quilting community have led to pieces with personal meaning. "Quilters on the Information Highway" is pieced from blocks called "Logon Cabin," houses with doors containing the names of each quilter, and telephone poles and wires connecting the blocks. The millennium quilt, stitched from 1,000 "charms," or pieces of cloth sent to her from around the country, was one of 24 selected for display at Houston's International Quilt Show, the largest in the United States.

Reynolds sees her work and quilting in general changing with the times. Once, women quilted to keep their families warm. The tradition waned when machine-made bed covers became easy to buy. Nostalgia generated by the 1976 Bicentennial sparked a revival, as people revisited quilting and found in it an art form. Reynolds also sees in quilting a deeper value. "It's like finding an ancient gene, a comfort that is missing in our modern bodies. We need to get back to that." ✱

48. TOMÉ ART GALLERY
Tomé, 2930 HWY 47

Along the Río Grande valley, just off a historic plaza, Tomé Gallery pays homage to longstanding local traditions like weaving and straw appliqué, while presenting outstanding contemporary work. Wander the rooms of this cozy adobe to find felted bags and hats, baskets, fiber sculpture, woven wearables and household items, jewelry, beaded pictures, handspun and dyed Churro yarn, and more. Visit with the artists who staff this cooperative gallery. There is almost always something happening in Tomé Gallery. Inquire about classes, workshops, and summer youth classes.

Chiricahua Gallery

Monte Cristo Gift Shop & Gallery
(Pioneer Store Museum)

T-SU, 10-5 505.565.0556
tomegallery.net
From I-25, Los Lunas exit, east to Hwy 47. Turn south on Hwy 47. Gallery is just north of mile marker 25 on Hwy 47, between Los Lunas and Belen. ●

49. PEPPERS GALLERY
Magdalena, 100 First Street

A historic house has been converted to be a showcase of local talent. See the work of over 20 area fiber artists, including weaving and beadwork from the nearby Alamo Navajo Reservation, woven rugs, shawls, and scarves of silk and chenille, felted hats, knitted and crocheted accessories, handmade paper, art baskets, quilts, and more, all under one roof.

TH-SU, 9-5 505.854.3696
peppersgallery.com
From I-25 in Socorro, Hwy 60 to Magdalena. Gallery is at mile marker 113, on right. ♿

50. MAGDALENA ARTS GALLERY
Magdalena, 602 HWY 60

Community is at the heart of this cooperative gallery, whose members work together running the store, hosting special events, and inspiring each other with new ideas. This bright, open space has had multiple incarnations as a car dealership, telephone office, beauty parlor, and feed store. Today, it showcases an amazing array of rugs, clothing, and yardage woven from local wool, framed batik on silk, and needle-felted scenes, quilts, knitted apparel, tie-dyed clothing, and more. New Mexico-made soy silk, mohair, and special blend yarns are sold here.

W-M, 10-4
505.854.3318
From I-25 in Socorro, Hwy 60 to Magdalena. Gallery is in town center on Hwy 60. ⚘

[SOUTH]

⚘ Supplies ● Classes and workshops ♿ Wheelchair accessible
♿ Wheelchair accessible restrooms ☎ Check road conditions

From top: Royal Fiber Spinnery; Tomé Gallery; Magdalena Arts Gallery.

woven from cotton, rayon, silk, linen, and metallics – in intricate patterns, light as air. Call to arrange large tours. The studio is also home of Hokett Would Work, producer of spinning and weaving tools and equipment.

W & TH, 10-2 505.854.3451
weaver_dancing
@yahoo.com
From I-25 in Socorro, Hwy 60 to Magdalena. In Magdalena, left onto Chestnut at WEAVING sign. Left at second stop sign. You will see CREATIONS sign outside the studio with turquoise French doors. ✂

51. HOLLY MODINE STUDIO
Magdalena, 460 Spruce

Holly Modine's baskets emanate from her vision that while baskets are an ancient, functional tradition, they are also an art form with sculptural possibilities. She combines reeds and seagrass – some dyed in vibrant colors – with materials gathered from the landscape around her home: branches, vines, antlers, and metal scraps. She delights in the tactile process of basketry, her hands working in partnership with her materials. "They have a life of their own – I'm just there to help them find it."

T & W, 10-4 505.854.2918
modinehollyj.com
From I-25 in Socorro, Hwy 60 to Magdalena. Left on Spruce St.; south 4.5 blocks. Studio is on right in Old School. ♿♿

52. CAT BRYSCH CREATIONS STUDIO
Magdalena,
100 Eighth Street

Step into this bright, open studio for a weaving education. With seven looms in continual production, Cat Brysch happily explains "The Life of a Thread" to visitors. Marvel at her exquisite yardage, stoles, and scarves

53. SHEPHERD STUDIOS
Datil, 11 Agua Fria Trail

It's a scenic drive to Jonille Shepherd's sun-filled studio and gallery. Take in stunning views of South Crosby Peak, the Black Range, and Plains of San Augustín. Her intricate weaving will appeal to your elegant and practical sides. Chenille shawls and scarves and felted hats, side by side with aprons woven in old-fashioned coverlet designs – classic. Visit in the summer, and you might just walk away with an armful of fresh herbs from Shepherd's abundant garden.

M & F, 12-4 505.772.5603
shepherd@gilanet.com
From Magdalena, west on Hwy 60 to Datil. Left on NM 12; travel 6 miles. Right on Wildwood Trail, a gravel road. After 1/2 mile, left on Agua Fria Trail. Go 1.5 miles. Studio on the left. ☎

✂ Supplies ● Classes and workshops ♿ Wheelchair accessible
♿ Wheelchair accessible restrooms ☎ Check road conditions

54. MONTE CRISTO GIFT SHOP & GALLERY
Chloride, Wall Street

Meander through grassy valleys and mountain vistas to a ghost town alive with art and history. Once the Monte Cristo Saloon and Dance Hall, this gallery features fiber art made by local hands. Felting, knitting, handmade paper, beadwork, spinning, quilting, rug hooking, weaving, miniatures, locally made knitting kits with handspun, hand-dyed yarn, and more. Next door, the town mercantile, a boarded-up time capsule for more than 70 years, is now a restored Pioneer Store Museum.

M-SU, 10-4 505.743.0493
montecristo@zianet.com
From I-25, exit 83, north of Truth or Consequences. North on Hwy 181. West on Hwy 52 to Winston. Take second left, stay on the paved road to Chloride, 2.5 miles to the west end of town. ⅗ ♿

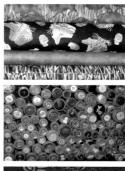

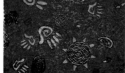

Thunder Creek Quilt Company
(all above).

TRES MANOS

Tres Manos

THE "THREE HANDS" OF TRES MANOS are its sponsor, the Community Action Agency of Southern New Mexico, the local community, and the women who weave in the San Miguel workshop. Program director Maria Navarra Pino jokes, "If anybody knows anything about weaving, they know you need three hands!" Since 2002, she has taught residents of local colonias on the U.S.-Mexico border the art of contemporary weaving, giving them a new and satisfying way to earn a living close to home, where the only alternative is working in the fields. Remarkably, none of the Tres Manos weavers ever wove before entering the program. From dressing the loom to developing her own color palette and designs, each woman has blossomed into an accomplished artist. With support from New Mexico Arts, the program's earliest participants help teach new weavers.

In 2006, Tres Manos weavers visited the New Mexico State Legislature, where they successfully rallied funds for their program. For many of the women, this was their first trip away from home. En route back from Santa Fe, one weaver inquired, "When are we going to Washington? The president needs to know about us." ✳

THE ANGORA QUEEN

MARGARET ARMER

MARGARET ARMER was a young woman and mother of six when widowed by her husband, an unsuccessful Sierra County miner.

The family's adopted angora goat provided milk, as well as inspiration that paved the way to better times. Armer (1863–1933) and her oldest son traded herding a neighbor's flock of 1,000 angoras for a share of their profits. Over time, she acquired the flock and bred it carefully, making it the largest in the U.S., while obtaining the finest mohair.

Her success and fame extended to the Chicago World's Fair, among other illustrious venues, and across the ocean: royalty from Russia and Pakistan bought her goats.

Thankful for the help the angora goats gave her family in difficult times, the woman who came to be known as the Angora Queen was able to put her sons through college, "to place them just as high in life as I can afford."

See mohair samples and Armer's trophies at the Geronimo Springs Museum in Truth or Consequences. ✳

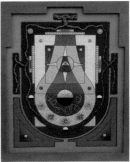

From left: Chiricahua Gallery; Tomé Art Gallery.

Grasshopper Silk

55. GRASSHOPPER SILK
Elephant Butte,
509 Bass Road

"Painting on silk keeps you thinking on your feet." Sandra Hopper delights in the free-flow way that steam-set dyes take on a life of their own when they meet up with silk, leading to abstract designs and vibrant colors. Learn firsthand about this complex process, which she teaches in private classes and workshops. Shop for hand-painted silk clothing or framed pieces.

SA & SU, 11-4 505.740.4958
grasshoppersilk.com
From I-25, exit 83, take Hwy 195 toward Hot Springs Landing. Turn left

on Rock Canyon Rd. at Valero station. Go 7/10 mile; turn right on Springland. At Hot Springs Landing Welcome sign, bear left onto Hot Springs Rd. Go 1/10 mile; turn right on Bass. Bright pink studio overlooks lake, 3.9 miles from I-25. ●

56. CELESTIAL CREATIONS
Truth or Consequences,
220 Date Street

Celeste Rich is dedicated to showcasing the work of area artists: "It's amazing, the amount of talent in Sierra County." Her emporium of local treasures astounds with its variety: Mescalero Apache beadwork, hand-pieced quilts, woven rugs and shawls, handmade paper cards, decorated gourds, crocheted work, and more.

M, T, TH-SA, 11-5; SU, 11-4
505.894.7591
celestial-creations-nm.com
From I-25, exit 79, which becomes Date St. Gallery is at corner of 2nd Ave. and Date. ♿

✂ Supplies ● Classes and workshops ♿ Wheelchair accessible
♿ Wheelchair accessible restrooms ☎ Check road conditions

57. GERONIMO SPRINGS MUSEUM
Truth or Consequences, 211 Main Street

This true community museum is chock-full of local treasures. Experience history through fiber: prehistoric woven sandals and baskets, Navajo blankets, beaded and sewn clothing, a quilt pieced from recycled tobacco sacks stitched with local cattle brands. Colorful vintage Fiesta dresses tell the story of the city's name. On April Fool's Day 1950, Hot Springs became Truth or Consequences for a day, honoring visiting television host Ralph Edwards with a Fiesta. Extravagant handmade outfits enlivened the celebration: tiered skirts from yards of fabric and miles of trim, with matching blouses. The name and the annual fiesta (now in May) stuck.

M-SA, 9-5; SU, 11-4
505.894.6600
geronimosprings
museum.com
From I-25 N, exit 75. Follow signs to museum. Left on Pershing St. to 211 Main St. From I-25 S, exit 79. Follow signs to Geronimo Springs Museum. &

Elemental Arts

58. PERCHA CREEK TRADERS CO-OP
Hillsboro, 300 Main Street

A cozy territorial adobe in the heart of Hillsboro's historic downtown. Fiber lovers will find stunning quilts, handmade dolls, lampshades crafted from handmade paper textured with native seeds, grasses, and flowers, and much more. Members staff this cooperative gallery, so you can visit with the artists. A gem in the heart of an old mining town.

W-SU, 10-4 505.895.5116
From I-25, exit 63 south of Truth or Consequences. Go 18 miles.

59. THE COMMON THREAD
Silver City, 107 Broadway

The heart of southern New Mexico's fiber arts community is home to the Southwest Women's Fiber Arts Collective. SWFAC is a nonprofit organization bridging rural isolation by providing mutual support for regional fiber artists to grow artistically and economically. Their classes and programs bring quality learning opportunities to local underserved populations. The common thread within this diverse group is their passion for fiber arts and a commitment to building more vibrant communities through creativity and connection. In their elegant Silver City gallery, more than 60 area artists show an astonishing array of work: hand-woven and knitted wearables, rugs, felted sculptures, petit point, handmade paper, colorful baskets, crochet, quilts, beaded headdresses, and more. Also available are handspun yarn, hand-dyed fat quarters and silk squares, and handmade buttons. Visit with the artists

[SOUTH]

From left: Elemental Arts; Hillsboro General Store Cafe.

HANDMADE IN NEW MEXICO

A MATTER OF VALUE

The Common Thread

THE NEW MEXICO FIBER ARTS TRAILS wind through remarkably varied ecosystems, cultural landscapes, and artistic practices. Whether their roots reach for generations into New Mexico soil or their hearts have brought them here from elsewhere, fiber artists statewide share a deep connection to place and the desire to make their art and a living where they live.

Customers sometimes balk at the price of a fiber arts piece, wondering, Why so expensive? In two words: time and dedication. Many local fiber artists process their own materials, spending many hours growing, harvesting, spinning, or dyeing, before they even begin a piece. Mastery of art forms and creative growth evolve over decades.

Handmade New Mexico fiber arts compete with inexpensive imports, with machine-made items, a discount mentality, and the notion that fiber arts are somehow less valuable than "fine" arts. Shelley Loveless of Rio Fernando Farm observes, "With modern technology, people lose track of where things come from."

"People think it's all done by magic because they just go to the store and buy things," says weaver Cat Brysch. But when she shares the process of her work, the response from visitors is often, "My goodness, your prices are not that high after all!"

What fiber artists do *is* magic when you consider the synergy of creativity, materials, and place. Learning firsthand what goes into a fiber art piece adds beauty – and value – to the eye of the beholder. Buying locally made fiber arts is an investment in one of New Mexico's most precious resources. You come away with something of enduring value to enjoy, and you support the creative heritage that makes our state an artistic gem. ✳

– they're the staff and regular droppers-by. SWFAC publishes an annual fiber artists' directory, emails members, and participates in several shows annually. Inquire about classes, volunteer opportunities, and fiber arts summer camp. ✂ ● ♿

M, TH-SA, 10-5 505.538.5733
fiberartscollective.org
info@fiberarts
collective.org

FIBER NETWORK SITE
Check with SWFAC for updates about southern Fiber Arts Trails sites.

60. ELEMENTAL ARTS
Silver City,
106 W Yankie Street

In the heart of Silver City's downtown Yankie-Texas Art District, step inside a light-filled space to find high quality art by local artists. It's elemental: fiber, clay, gourds, and feathers, celebrating the earth's bounty and the creative spirit. The focus is contemporary: fabulous gourd masks and sculptures by proprietor Valerie Milner. Woven, quilted, and surface-adorned pieces, among other genres.

M-SA, 10-4; SU, 10-1
505.590.7554
gourdweb.com

Monte Cristo Gift Shop & Gallery
(Pioneer Store Museum)

From top: Thunder Creek Quilt Company; Galeria 200.

61. YADA YADA YARN
Silver City, 614 N Bullard

"Art & Conversation: a gallery and gathering space." Yada Yada Yarn lives up to its moniker: warm and inviting and full of beautiful yarns, knitting and crochet tools, books, art work, and a comfy nook where locals and visitors alike drop in to hang out, work on projects, and learn new stitches. Stop by for open knitting, crochet, spinning, and kids' sessions.

✄ ● ⅃ ♿

W-M, 11-5; M Evenings, 6:30-9 505.388.3350
yadayadayarn.com

62. THUNDER CREEK QUILT COMPANY Silver City, 1330 N Hudson

Fabric heaven! Thunder Creek is itself a crazy quilt of fabrics, notions, kits, patterns, and books. Multi-talented mother-daughter team Nancy Coryell and Cindy Ugarte keep a workshop in the store, where they piece and design quilts in those few and far between

MEDITATIONS ON THE BENEFITS OF HANDWORK

WE ARE LIVING IN a time when handwork is gaining momentum. Ever wonder why? Ask many fiber artists what they love about their work and they will mention its meditative quality.

Perhaps Maria Navarra Pino of Tres Manos puts it best: "We have evolved more technologically than we have physically or biologically. People don't even come out of their homes, doing all their work on the computer. And they're dying of isolation. Doing handwork makes you feel connected to yourself and to other people, to something real." ✳

Holly Modine Studio

[SOUTH]

Thunder Creek Quilt Company

64. CHIRICAHUA GALLERY
Rodeo, HWY 80

A historic building that has evolved from frontier saloon to church to its present incarnation as an art gallery is now the home of the longstanding Chiricahua Guild. It is worth every scenic mile of the drive to see high quality work by artists from a 100-mile radius at a gallery displaying a diversity of fiber arts: weaving, basketry, crochet, felting, knitting, embroidery, quilting, and gourd art. The Chiricahua Gallery is aptly named. Gaze through mottled antique glass windows at the constant play of light across the Chiricahua Mountains.

M-SA, 10-4 505.557.2225
winjac12@vtc.net
From Silver City, take Hwy 90 south. I-10 west. At Road Forks, take Hwy 80 south to Rodeo. Gallery is on left in historic church building.

quiet moments. Their fine handwork abounds in every corner. Specialty: southwestern fabrics. Also available: one-on-one instruction, long-arm quilting, and, yes, sewing machine repair. ✂ ●

M-F, 9-5; SA, 10-4
505.538.2284
sneezweeds@zianet.com

63. DOC CAMPBELL'S POST/ GILA COUNTRY CORNER GALLERY
Gila Hot Springs,
Mile marker 39 HWY 15

Steeped in local history, Doc Campbell's Post harks back to a family tradition of hospitality that began in 1940, when the Campbell family bought the Gila Hot Springs Ranch. In the upstairs gallery, shop for a wide variety of locally made fiber arts: knitted clothing from silk and wool (including yarn spun from the resident flock of Churros), felted bags and hats, beadwork, mixed media, woven, crocheted and quilted items. Enjoy spectacular

views of the Gila Wilderness and delicious homemade ice cream!

Memorial Day Weekend –Labor Day, 8:30-5; Winter, 10-4 505.536.9551
gilahotspringsranch.com
From Silver City, go 39 miles north on Hwy 15. Store is on right. Note: 39 miles as the crow flies, but Hwy 15 wends its way over a winding route. Allow at least 1.5 hours to travel, preferably in daylight. ☎ ♿

Left and right: The Common Thread.

✂ Supplies ● Classes and workshops ♿ Wheelchair accessible
♿ Wheelchair accessible restrooms ☎ Check road conditions

STITCHING CIRCUMSTANCE INTO BEAUTY

UNIVERSAL ACROSS the United States, quilting has its own flavor in New Mexico.

During the last quarter of the 19th century, the railroad and mail-order catalogs brought fabric to northern New Mexico, where weaving had long prevailed as a source of warm bed covers. Quilting evolved organically as an economic alternative, often incorporating Hispanic aesthetics in the outer layers, and recycled weaving materials like wool blankets, clothing, or carded wool inside as batting.

In southern New Mexico, traditional quilting designs and techniques from the eastern United States took root as Anglo settlers made the area their home.

Over time, distinctions between northern and southern quilting tapered off, as ease of travel and published quilting patterns fueled mutual influence. The common thread has always been thrift combined with personal expression, as quilters pieced whatever might be on hand – tobacco pouches, flour sacks, clothing, and remnants – to beautify their homes or pad bedrolls.

Today, New Mexico quilters tend toward machine piecing and quilting with new fabrics. Hand piecing and quilting are often the province of elders or devotees of historical quilting.

Contemporary art quilts have joined the ranks of practical bed covers. Visit a local county fair or quilt show and you'll see enduring favorites like Log Cabin

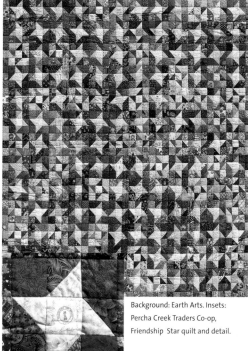

Background: Earth Arts. Insets: Percha Creek Traders Co-op, Friendship Star quilt and detail.

or Dresden Plate. Just as likely, you'll encounter designs inspired by Hispanic or Native American weaving, pottery or rock art motifs, depictions of mountainous landscapes, desert creatures like roadrunners or horned toads, chile ristras, and hot air balloons, as well as abstract or contemporary designs.

Throughout the state, the abundance of quilting guilds attests to the art form's unwavering popularity as a way to build community and share ideas, whether on the latest technique or a civic issue. Once isolated by geography and the demands of agricultural work, quilters continue to embrace the need to gather as a refuge from the demands of hectic lives. ✳

65. GALERIA 200
Deming, 200 S Gold Street

Artists Lyn and Richard Orona long dreamed of having their own gallery. Their dream-come-true is now a boon for local artists, who have a beautiful place to market their work. In a lovingly restored historic building in the heart of a railroad town, you will find hand-painted silk clothing, southwestern gourd masks and bowls, woven pieces for your home, and art quilts like none you've ever seen before.

TU-F, 10-5; SA, 10-4
505.546.9590
galeria200.com
From I-10, exit 82. South on Hwy 180/Gold St. At second traffic light, look for a red brick building on southwest corner. ♿

66. TRES MANOS BOUTIQUE
Mesilla,
1910 Calle de Parian

The Tres Manos boutique charms a corner of Mesilla's old tortilla factory, a short walk from the historic Plaza. A dazzling array of shawls, scarves, clothing, and rugs, woven in a multitude of colors and patterns from cotton, tencel, silk, chenille, hand-dyed bouclé, and more await you in this elegant store. Delight the senses with rich colors and textures – the "Oooh!" factor is high at Tres Manos.

SA, SU, 10-5 505.524.2334
tresmanossm@hotmail.com
From I-10, exit 140, Avenida de Mesilla, also Hwy 28, turn south. The old tortilla factory housing Tres Manos boutique is on the right.

67. TRES MANOS WORKSHOP
San Miguel, 19030 HWY 28

South of Mesilla, across the Río Grande, through cotton and chile fields and an enchanting pecan grove, San Miguel is home to the Tres Manos workshop. Stop by and visit the dedicated and talented weavers whose work graces the boutique (see entry above). Each artist has her own style, her own eye for color and design. The common denominator among this congenial group is friendship and a high standard of quality, strictly enforced by the weavers themselves.

Clockwise from top left: Unravel Yarn Shop & Gallery; Magdalena Arts Gallery; The Common Thread; Galeria 200.

M-F, 8-4 505.233.1106.
tresmanossm@hotmail.com
From Mesilla, go 10 miles south on Hwy 28. In San Miguel, the Youth Art Development Building is on your left. ♿

68. UNRAVEL YARN SHOP & GALLERY
Las Cruces,
300 N Downtown Mall

Unravel your cares at this cozy corner brimming with local materials and talent. Everything you need for your next project is right here: dazzling yarns, tools, books, classes, and a friendly, knowledgeable staff who will help retrieve dropped stitches.

✂ Supplies ● Classes and workshops ♿Wheelchair accessible
♿Wheelchair accessible restrooms ☎ Check road conditions

M, TU, TH, F, 10-5; W, 9-5;
SA, 9-4   505.647.1181
unravel-yarn-shop.com
*From I-25, take the Lohman
St. exit. West on Lohman.
Right on Campo. Left on Las
Cruces. First block on right.*
✄ ● ⚭ ♿

69. NEW MEXICO FARM AND RANCH HERITAGE MUSEUM
Las Cruces,
4100 Dripping Springs Rd

Spacious grounds have
open-air livestock and farming displays and a splendid
view of the Organ Mountains.
Compelling permanent and
rotating exhibits – many
with bilingual signage –
explore the state's agricultural
heritage and interweave
of cultures, from prehistoric
times to the present at this
New Mexico Department of
Cultural Affairs museum.
Wednesday mornings from
9 to noon, local artists
demonstrate spinning, weaving,
quilting, and sewing. Gift
shop and restaurant add to
the experience.

M-SA, 9-5; SU, 12-5
505.522.4100 frhm.org
*From I-25, take University
exit. Go 1.5 miles east on
University, which becomes
Dripping Springs Rd. Museum
is on left.* ● ⚭ ♿

The Common Thread

BEAUTIFYING LIFE

CASSIE HOBBS

Cassie Hobbs, Monte Cristo Gift Shop & Gallery (Pioneer Store Museum).

"CASSIE HOBBS WAS QUITE A LADY, emphasis on
the word lady," Linda Turner, of Monte Cristo Gift Shop
& Gallery, remembers her inspiring neighbor.

Hobbs traveled to New Mexico with her family via
covered wagon from Oklahoma and Texas. When she
and her husband, Earl, a cowboy, settled in Chloride,
she not only hoisted the beams for their living room but
also furnished their home with her own hand-hewn
furniture, and stitched upholstery, linens, and clothing
to beautify their lives.

Over a life of frequent moves, Hobbs (1904–1989)
used simple tools and her ingenuity to craft furnishings
from found and recycled materials.

Among her mind-boggling creations are handmade
shoes, carved from wood and covered in crocheted lace,
with handbags and bonnets to match. Embroidery,
hand-tailored clothing, crochet, appliqué, and many
other handmade items are her legacy, telling the story of
a spirited pioneer woman. See these treasures at the
Pioneer Store Museum in Chloride. ✳

[SOUTH]

70. ROYAL FIBER SPINNERY
Ruidoso, 815 Gavilan
Canyon Road

Rod and Marilyn Dakan
have made it their business
to make high-quality alpaca
available to knitters, crocheters,
and weavers nationwide.
Imagine: five weights of
yarn in over 100 natural
and hand-dyed colors! Take
a guided tour of the farm
and mill – one of the largest
U.S. processors of alpaca.
Visit cuddly alpacas and see
every step of the work from
fleece to finished yarn, and
indulge your yarn addiction
in a rainbow of a showroom.

TU-TH, 10-4 505.258.9276
(yarn) rstoreonline.com
*Gavilan Rd. can be accessed
from Hwy 48 or Hwy 70
(Sudderth Rd.) in Ruidoso.
The mill is well marked on
west side of the road.* ✂ ♿ 🚻

71. ZW'S GALLERY
Nogal, 109 Red Fox

Nancie Ferguson grew up
on a Wisconsin dairy farm
where, she says, "We re-used
everything." Ferguson
upholds the recycling tradition, weaving colorful and
sturdy rugs from Pendleton
loom selvages or bluejeans left
on her porch by neighbors. This

working studio also carries her
double-walled, Cherokee-style
baskets, quilts, rugs, and runners
woven from her own homespun,
and brooms she weaves from
broom corn for her blacksmith
husband's fireplace sets.

TH & F, 12-5 505.354.4263
zwsoo@yahoo.com
*Hwy 37 between Ruidoso and
Carrizozo, between mile markers
4 and 5 on the east side of Hwy
37. Closer to Ruidoso than
Carrizozo.*

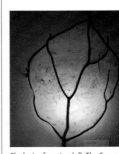

Clockwise from top left: The Common
Thread; Doc Campbell's Post/Gila
Country Corner Gallery; The Common
Thread; Percha Creek Traders Co-op;
Chiricahua Gallery.

✂ Supplies   ● Classes and workshops   ♿ Wheelchair accessible
🚻 Wheelchair accessible restrooms   ☎ Check road conditions

STRENGTH IN NUMBERS

Background: Terrazas Traditional Arts. From top: Koehler
Studio; Española Valley Fiber Arts Center.

NEW MEXICO FIBER ARTISANS
(NMFA) was born from the same collective momentum that launched the New
Mexico Fiber Arts Trails. NMFA makes a
vital connection among fiber artists and
fiber arts activities statewide.

In 2005, New Mexico Arts brought
Handmade in America's rural arts and
heritage visionary Becky Anderson to
explore possibilities for rural economic
development among New Mexico's artists.
Her contagious positive energy lit a spark
among representatives from ten fiber arts
organizations statewide, who recognized
the unique assets among their diverse
communities, as well as the benefits of
collaboration.

A network of kindred spirits then
galvanized to become New Mexico Fiber
Artisans. The group's charter is to support
fiber arts wherever they are, in all the
wonderful far-flung corners of the state
where creativity thrives in centuries-old
traditions and cutting-edge contemporary

work. Arts Enterprise Partnerships funding
from New Mexico Arts contributes to
those efforts.

NMFA has blossomed into an organization of 100 members and growing, with
inclusiveness and diversity a strength upon
which to build. Fiber artists, non-profit
organizations, businesses, mills, galleries,
artists' co-ops, museums, schools, farms,
and gardens – each has something to contribute and something to learn. Collectively,
fiber artists from around the state share
their thoughts, ideas, opportunities, and
expertise to bridge New Mexico's wide
open spaces. The nascent organization
promotes mutual support, through which
new opportunities for marketing, self-sufficiency, artistic growth, and stewardship
of our precious resources will benefit all.

Founding NMFA member Diane
Bowman writes, "It is our vision to encompass the entire state with a structure of
support, encouragement, and economic
opportunity for fiber artisans . . . and for
visitors to experience the unbroken
connection between the land, culture, and
creativity that we are blessed with in
New Mexico."

New Mexico Fiber Artisans maintains
a mailing list, online discussion group,
and member directory. Learn more at
nmfiberartisans.org, or at 505.747.3577
in northern New Mexico, or 505.538.5733
in the south. ✳

Shooting Star Farm

TRAILS SITES IN ALPHABETICAL ORDER

NEW MEXICO FIBER ARTS TRAILS

GLOSSARY

ALPACA Gentle fiber animals native to the Andes, of growing popularity in New Mexico. Alpaca fleeces vary in color, and the yarn is exceptionally warm, soft, and durable, which may be why alpacas were once exclusively owned by Incan royalty. Learn more about them at *newmexicoalpacabreeders.org.*

ANGORA Angora goats are thought to have originated in the Himalayas but take their name from the Ankara region of Turkey, where they were prized for the strong, lustrous mohair yarn spun from their fleece, which grows about an inch a month. Angora rabbits are lovable creatures whose silky fur – seven times warmer than sheep's wool – is often spun with other fibers. Angora fur is plucked or clipped and spun into angora yarn.

BATTING The inside layer of a quilt, fixed with quilted or tied stitches between the top and bottom layers. The batting of a quilt provides its warmth.

BULLPEN A product of their time, historic trading posts were modeled after old-time general stores, where socializing was a key ingredient of trade. Merchandise was stacked to the ceiling on shelves behind a three-sided counter, leaving the area beyond – the bullpen – for customers to visit, sip coffee, and trade.

CHURRO The breed of sheep brought to New Mexico by the Spanish in the late 16th century. Churro fleeces occur in many beautiful natural colors – sometimes on the same sheep! Over the centuries, Churros, once the prevalent Southwest breed, became scarce. In recent years, they are making a comeback in New Mexico, where they are cherished as fiber animals for their easily spun, double-coated fleece and for their roots in local heritage (*navajo churrosheep.com* and *navajolifeway.org*).

COLCHA Colcha is Spanish for "bed cover," as it was used in Spanish colonial households. Colcha also refers to the actual stitch and the style of embroidery; the latter is unique to New Mexico and southern Colorado. Traditionally, colcha was done with handspun, naturally dyed yarn on a hand-woven woolen cloth. With the advent of manufactured cloth, yarn, and dyes, these more painstaking techniques waned but have been revived in recent years by artists dedicated to preserving the traditional approach. Colcha is often stitched in floral or bird motifs onto altar cloths or other household items.

FAT QUARTER Literally, a quarter of a yard of fabric cut "fat," or square, as opposed to long and thin, giving a more usable dimension for most quilters. "FQ's," generally 22" wide x 18" high, allow quilters to add to their stash economically and are easily traded, given away, or sent through the mail. FQ bins are a staple at fabric stores and quilting festivals.

FELTING A process by which woolen fabric is soaked and agitated in soapy water to shrink and mat it, joining the fibers together to make felt.

JERGA In colonial northern New Mexico, jerga was a thick cloth woven from wool yarn on a four-harness loom in twill weave patterns – checks, plaids, or diamonds, or *ojo de perdiz*, "partridge eye." Jerga was used for floor coverings, sack cloth, and clothing.

GLOSSARY

LLAMA The ancient ancestors of llamas migrated from North America to South America, where they were prized by the Incans as pack animals and for the fiber produced from their fleece. Llama fiber varies in color – black, white, and shades of brown, red, and gray – and in fiber, from fine to coarse.

MANTA Manta is Spanish for "blanket" – in the Southwest, a term with multiple meanings. Manta refers to small blankets woven historically by both Pueblo and Navajo people to wear as dresses or shawls. Before the arrival of sheep in the Southwest, mantas were woven from cotton on upright looms. Mantas varied widely in appearance, woven in plain or fancy weaves, with woven, embroidered, or painted designs. They are still worn today in Pueblo ceremonials.

NATURAL DYES Colors derived from natural materials to dye fiber that is used in traditional and contemporary fiber arts. Some plant sources include indigo for blue; madder for orange or red-brown; chamisa and *cota*, or Navajo tea, for yellow; and black walnut for brown. Dyes made from insects include cochineal for reds and pinks and lac for red.

NAVAJO BASKETS Coiled Navajo baskets are traditionally woven from sumac and willow in the red and black, stepped "wedding" design. These baskets enjoy continued use in ceremonials and are also valued by collectors. In recent years, basket weavers have added pictorial baskets to the repertoire, creating designs with animals, flowers, and scenes from Navajo life and history in a multitude of colors.

RÍO GRANDE WEAVING DESIGN SYSTEMS

RÍO GRANDE The design that took root in New Mexico with the earliest Spanish settlers in the late-16th century, consisting of banded stripes of alternating color, sometimes designs within the stripes.

SALTILLO Entering the Río Grande repertoire in the early 1900s, inspired by blankets from Saltillo, Mexico. Serrated diamonds are its hallmark, usually in a central motif, often with vibrant design elements in the background or corners. Variations abound.

VALLERO A symmetrical eight-pointed star, often with one large motif in the center of a piece and smaller stars in the corners or borders.

CHIMAYÓ Originating in the early 20th century, Chimayó designs have striped borders at either end, with central diamond motifs that are used in recognizable variation. In addition to rugs and blankets, other items such as wool pillows, throws, jackets, purses, and vests are also woven in Chimayó designs.

ROVING A continuous rope of slightly twisted fiber, made in preparation for spinning.

RUANA A long shawl open in the front.

SABANILLA Wool yardage woven on a treadle loom as ground cloth for colcha embroidery.

SPINNING The process of simultaneously drawing out and twisting fiber into a continuous strand to create yarn. In New Mexico, handspinning is accomplished on a traditional Hispanic malacate or Navajo spindle, or on a spinning wheel. The resulting yarn is homespun or handspun.